H1

D0238883

Adult Education
The Challenge of Change

Report by a Committee of Inquiry
appointed by the Secretary of State for Scotland
under the Chairmanship of Professor K J W Alexander

Scottish Education Department

Her Majesty's Stationery Office   Edinburgh   1975

ISBN 0 11 491308 0

Contents

Foreword
BY THE SECRETARY OF STATE

This Report deals comprehensively with the present position of adult education in Scotland, the aims which it might seek to attain in the future, and how these aims might be achieved. It has been awaited with great interest, not only by those engaged in adult education but also by those concerned directly and indirectly with community education in the widest sense. It makes many important recommendations which will have to be examined carefully by the Government, the education authorities and the other interests involved.

I shall be consulting all these interests before reaching decisions on the recommendations.

I am sure that my gratitude to Professor Alexander and his colleagues for the thorough and imaginative way in which they have carried out their work is shared by all those concerned with the provision of adult education in Scotland.

WILLIAM ROSS

Introduction

Dear Secretary of State

We were appointed in May 1970 with the following terms of reference:

'To consider the aims appropriate to voluntary leisure time courses for adults which are educational but not specifically vocational; to examine the extent to which these are being achieved at present; and with due regard to the need to use available resources most effectively, to make recommendations.'

Unfortunately two of the original members of our Committee were unable to remain with us throughout our work. Councillor R Pirie found at a very early stage that the pressures of his civic duties prevented him from attending our meetings and he tendered his resignation. Mr K A Wood was appointed in his stead. Mr M Baillie, for personal domestic reasons, has not been able to attend meetings since May 1971. In the circumstances he takes the view that it would be inappropriate for him to sign the report.

I have very much pleasure in presenting our report. While it represents the views of the Committee generally, Mr M T Sweeney was unable to agree the recommendations relating to the Workers' Educational Association. His Note of Dissent is included as an addendum to the report.

The Committee have met on 24 occasions and in addition, there have been many meetings of the various sub-committees we found it necessary to set up to deal with specific matters.

We received written evidence from 105 organisations and individuals and oral evidence from 31 (see Appendices XVIII and XIX). We are most grateful to all of them for their readiness to help us in our task and for answering our questions.

Members of the Committee in groups visited many areas, institutions etc both in the United Kingdom and overseas (see Appendix XX) and had discussions with officials, members of staff, students and many others involved in adult education. To everyone who helped to make these visits and discussions possible we offer our sincere thanks for all their trouble and for the unfailing kindness we received wherever we went.

We wish to express our appreciation of the help given to us by the Education Authorities of Argyll, Dundee and Fife and the Extra-Mural Departments of the Universities of Dundee, Edinburgh, Glasgow and St Andrews who co-operated in carrying out case studies in these three areas on our behalf, the results of which were very helpful to us; and our thanks to Mr Norman Dees, Director of Extra-Mural Studies and Adult Education, University of Glasgow, who directed the studies.

We also wish to record our gratitude to Professor H A Jones, University of Leicester, and Mr G J Brown, HMI, Scottish Education Department, for their advice and assistance; and to the late Mr John Eaton, Senior Lecturer in Mathematics, University of Strathclyde, whose work on our behalf in connection with the collation and analysis of statistical material was interrupted by his sudden death. This work was taken over, at very short notice, by Mr Ian Grant, Lecturer in Statistics, Civil Service College, Edinburgh, to whom we are also deeply indebted.

We are, Sir
Your obedient Servants
K J W ALEXANDER
Chairman
(on behalf of the Committee)

MEMBERSHIP OF COMMITTEE

Professor K J W Alexander (Chairman) Professor of Economics, University of Strathclyde

Dr D Dickson CB (Vice-Chairman) Formerly Her Majesty's Senior Chief Inspector, Scottish Education Department

Mr M Baillie (to 11 5 71) Tutor (Fine Art), Department of Adult Education and Extra-Mural Studies, University of Glasgow

Mr J T Bain Director of Education, Glasgow

Mr A Cameron Teacher of Social Studies in Further Education, Glasgow

Mr N Chalmers Headteacher, Ainslie Park Secondary School, Edinburgh

Dr A P Curran Senior Lecturer, Department of Epidemiology and Preventive Medicine, University of Glasgow

Mr T P Gorrie County Treasurer, Dumfriesshire County Council

Mr J Kane OBE Secretary, South-East Scotland District, Workers' Educational Association

Mr W F Lindsay Director of Education, Moray and Nairn

Dr J Lowe Director, Department of Educational Studies, University of Edinburgh

Mr R C MacLean Director of Audio-Visual Services, Universities of Glasgow and Strathclyde

Mr R G McLeod OBE Principal, Telford College of Further Education, Edinburgh

Mr J P Murdoch TD Group Education and Training Manager, British Steel Corporation, Motherwell (retired 17 3 72)

Mrs T P D Murray MBE Chairman, Angus Education Committee. Former Chairman of the Scottish Women's Rural Institutes

Mr R Pirie (to 2 5 71) Chairman, Aberdeen City Education Committee

Mr J P H Round Principal Lecturer in Youth and Community Services, Jordanhill College of Education

Mr M T Sweeney Regional Education Officer, Trades Union Congress, Glasgow

Miss J Vaughan Social Worker, Midlothian County Council Social Work Department

Mr K A Wood (from 18 6 71) Director, Department of Adult Education and Extra-Mural Studies, University of Aberdeen

Mr D W Young Warden, Palace of Art, Bellahouston, Glasgow (retired 8 3 74)

ASSESSORS
Mr J Kidd Scottish Education Department

HMI Mr D S Graham Scottish Education Department

HMI Mr D McCalman (from 26 1 73) Scottish Education Department

SECRETARY
Mr D R McFarlane Scottish Education Department

Summary of Recommendations

Definition
1. 'Adult', for adult education purposes should be held to mean any person over statutory school leaving age (Para 3).

Statutory Responsibility
2. Statutory responsibility for adult education provision should continue to be vested solely in the education authorities (Para 160).

Community Education Service and Council
3. Adult education should be regarded as an aspect of community education and with the youth and community service, should be incorporated into a community education service (Para 94).

4. The Secretary of State should establish a Scottish Council for Community Education (Para 164).

Organisation and Development
5. There should be on the staff of each education authority an officer of at least Assistant Director of Education grade with the sole responsibility for securing adequate provision of adult education (Para 174).

6. Regional advisory councils for community education should be set up in all education authority areas (Para 208). The initiative in setting them up should be taken by the education authorities who should also assume responsibility for servicing and financing them (Para 210).

7. Once decisions have been taken on our recommendations as to the future form of adult education, the Secretary of State should from time to time invite the education authorities to inform him of their plans for development along the agreed lines (Para 97).

8. The service must be expanded and the aim should be to double the number of students by the mid 1980s (Para 100).

Special Provision
9. There must be expanded provision for special groups of adults of all kinds including:
   (a) young mothers (Para 103);
   (b) the elderly (Para 104);
   (c) those with literacy problems (Para 109);
   (d) immigrants (Para 107);
   (e) inmates of penal establishments (Para 114);
   (f) the physically and mentally handicapped (Para 123);
   (g) those working unsocial hours (Para 106).

10. The elderly should be encouraged to become involved in adult education and community activities which provide them with opportunities for social contacts (Para 105).

11. It must be an important part of any after-care service for persons released from detention that those who have made educational progress while in detention should be put in contact with appropriate agencies with a view to maintaining their interest and motivation (Para 111).

12. Education authorities should be required to compile and maintain, in co-operation with social work departments and other appropriate organisations a register of all handicapped persons in their areas in order to establish their educational needs and ensure that these are met (Para 123).

13. In the deployment of resources high priority should be given to the needs of areas of multiple deprivation (Para 124).

14. In devising new approaches to contemporary social problems, including anti-social behaviour, it is essential to forge the strongest possible links between the social worker and the community educator (Para 135).

15. Provision in a wide range of Scottish traditional and cultural subjects should be increased (Para 130).

16. In Gaelic-speaking areas Gaelic should be used as a medium for some subjects in adult programmes (Para 131).

17. In determining their policies in relation to class sizes education authorities should be sympathetic to and understanding of the position of minority interest groups (Para 255).

Rural Areas
18. Such minima as are established in relation to class sizes should have full regard to population density and distribution and other conditions in the relevant area (Para 125).

19. Education authorities with special problems of remote and isolated

communities should examine the possibility of arranging for correspondence courses (Para 129).

20. In areas of isolated communities and transport difficulties consideration should be given to provision in the form of whole-day courses: and in such areas arrangements should be made in appropriate circumstances for the provision of transport, without cost to the student, between his home and his local adult education centre (Para 128).

21. In rural areas local part-time leadership should be identified and given responsibility for discovering suitable local personnel and accommodation able to assist in making adult education provision and for assisting in securing such provision and stimulating new interests. They should be given relevant in-service training and be appropriately paid (Para 127).

Resources and Accommodation
22. Careful stock should be taken of available resources for adult education and a strategy developed for their use (Para 221).

23. Accommodation specially designed for adult and general community use should be provided as extensions to local primary schools which have a reasonably assured future (Para 127).

24. Where school accommodation is used for adult education purposes steps should be taken to ensure that it is suitable for such use and free from inhibiting restrictions. Specialised school accommodation should be made freely available for adult purposes (Para 215).

25. Wherever possible community centres and adult centres should be used for adult education purposes and care should be taken to make them attractive to adults (Para 217).

26. Greater use should be made of colleges of further education for adult education purposes (Para 219).

Libraries, Museums, Art Galleries
27. Education authorities should consider with those responsible for libraries, museums and galleries in their areas how the resources of these institutions might more extensively be used in the interests of adult education (Para 203).

28. Library authorities should appoint appropriate members of staff to maintain close liaison with those concerned with adult education in their areas with a view to ensuring that the full resources of the library service are used in the interests of adult education (Para 199).

29. Libraries, museums and galleries should be represented on regional advisory councils for adult education (Para 203).

30. The development of touring exhibitions and mobile exhibitions of pictures and museum objects should be encouraged (Para 202).

Television and Radio
31. There should be a 4th TV channel (Para 146) but it should not be devoted exclusively to educational programmes (Para 147).

32. The additional channel should be based on the BBC (Para 148).

33. Two new national bodies concerned with the administration of educational broadcasting should be set up by Government, one should have executive functions to determine educational programme policy, and the allocation of programme time and the other 'watchdog' functions (Para 151).

Role of Universities
34. The universities should develop a community development approach in stimulating demand for adult education (Para 176).

35. Education authorities and regional advisory councils should support university staff appointments designed to encourage the promotion and organisation of adult education and the wider use in the adult education field of the intellectual and teaching talent in the universities (Para 177).

36. The universities should explore the possibility of introducing arrangements under which courses for particular professional groups oriented towards the professional interests of their members might be linked with the acquisition of recognised professional or academic qualifications. They should also consider offering certificates or diplomas for the successful completion of particular trends and levels of courses (Para 178).

37. The participation of all Scottish universities is desirable if the proposed expansion of the service is to be achieved (Para 179).

Workers' Educational Association
38. The Workers' Educational Association should concentrate its efforts on promoting the educational needs of the socially, economically and educationally disadvantaged and the education authorities should seek the help of the WEA in making the relevant provision (Para 185).

Voluntary organisations
39. Voluntary organisations should be encouraged to seek grant aid from the Scottish Education Department for developmental projects (Para 194).

Scottish Institute of Adult Education
40. The Scottish Institute of Adult Education should reconsider its constitution and functions in the changing situation and on this basis should continue to receive financial support from the Scottish Education Department (Para 196).

HM Inspectors
41. The number and qualifications of HM Inspectors with responsibilities in the community education field should be reviewed now in the light

of the changes proposed and should be reviewed regularly thereafter (Para 222).

Staff and Training

42. To secure the proposed development 200 additional full-time staff will be required over the next 5 years. The Government, the education authorities, and the voluntary organisations concerned should adopt this target and give priority to its achievement (Para 226).

43. The provision of an attractive career structure with opportunities for movement within the wider community service is essential to recruitment and development (Para 227).

44. The professional training needs of the service and of its various branches should be reviewed at regular intervals by the Scottish Council for Community Education (Para 230).

45. All persons seeking a career in adult education should be required to undergo an appropriate course of training (Para 231).

46. There should be elements of common training in the different courses of training for the various branches of the community education service and for social work (Para 235).

47. The Diploma in Adult Education courses at the Universities of Edinburgh and Glasgow should be expanded and developed (Para 232).

48. Arrangements for in-service training for full-time staff should be introduced. The universities and the colleges of education should co-operate with employing bodies in making the necessary provision (Para 234).

49. The universities and colleges of education should consider the inclusion of adult education as an option in the initial training courses for teachers and at special subject level in at least some B Ed degree structures. In time every B Ed course should include an appreciation of the purpose, characteristics and problems of adult education (Para 236).

50. Education authorities should be required, as a matter of urgency, to make available training facilities for part-time staff (Para 237).

51. The principle of incentive payments related to training should be extended (Para 238).

52. Education authorities should co-operate in devising improved scales of fees and allowances for part-time teachers (Para 242).

Trade Union Education

53. The teaching institutions and the trades unions should co-operate in securing an expansion of shop steward training. Greater use should be made of the Trades Union Congress Education Service as the point of contact between them in the planning and content of courses (Para 190).

54. The possibility of establishing a residential college and regional centre for industrial relations training should be explored by the Scottish Education Department in consultation with other interested parties (Para 191).

Other Residential Centres
55. Newbattle Abbey College should continue to be supported by both central and local government (Para 207).

56. Education authorities should consider the establishment, individually or collectively, of a centre or centres for short-term residential adult education courses etc. The new region of Strathclyde should establish its own such centre or centres (Para 206).

Finance
57. Action should be taken within the rate support grant system to ensure that any additional resources made available to education authorities for the development of adult education are applied to that purpose (Para 98).

58. The arrangement under which the Secretary of State makes grants under the Further Education (Scotland) Regulations 1959 to approved associations engaged in adult education towards their administration costs should be continued. The Workers' Educational Association should continue to be regarded as eligible for such grants and the extra-mural departments of the universities should be recognised as approved associations for the purpose (Para 211).

59. A new scheme of grants should be instituted by the Secretary of State for Scotland with the object of enabling approved associations to initiate developmental programmes (Para 212).

60. Fees should continue to be charged for adult education classes and courses (Para 246). The future fee structure should be sufficiently flexible to encourage expansion, development and the involvement of a greater number and wider range of students. There should be provision for the remission or waiving of fees for certain categories of students (Para 253).

61. Education authorities should be encouraged to make more extensive use of their statutory powers to provide financial assistance to adult education students (Para 266).

Paid Educational Leave
62. HM Government should introduce a scheme of incentives to encourage employers to grant paid leave to their employees to attend adult education classes and courses (Para 260).

Student Representation
63. Whenever student numbers make it practicable to do so an adult centre should establish (a) a management council which includes representatives of staff and students (Para 261); and (b) a students' association (Para 262).

Counselling
64. Education authorities should secure the establishment of an effective counselling service (Para 140) and an information and advisory service (Para 140).

Statistics
65. The question of the kind of statistics required for the development of an efficient adult service should be considered by the new Council (Para 42).

Research
66. There should be an expansion of research into aspects of adult education (Para 142).

PART I

1 Definition of Terms

1.   We first considered the implications of our remit. It refers to 'voluntary leisure time courses for adults which are educational but not specifically vocational'. We have taken this to mean courses of the kind which for many years have been widely known as adult education courses. The term 'adult education' does not appear in any of the Education (Scotland) Acts, and it has never been statutorily defined. It appears to have been used officially for the first time in the United Kingdom in 1919 when a Committee (known as the Smith Committee) appointed by the then Ministry of Reconstruction was given the task of considering 'the provision for, and the possibilities of, adult education (other than technical or vocational) in Great Britain' and of making recommendations.

2.   Although the term has been in common use since then we do not consider that it adequately describes the service as it is evolving nor do we see it as a suitable descriptive title for the service we envisage for the future. Social, cultural, recreational and educational activities for adults are so inter-related that any attempt to distinguish between them or to deal with one without regard to the others would be undesirable even if it were possible. This view of ours is reinforced by the increasing use of the term 'community education' to refer to the educational opportunities available to the individual through social, cultural, recreational and educational provision by statutory authorities and voluntary agencies, and through involvement in the numerous voluntary groups in the community. In our report we use the term 'community education' in this wide and comprehensive sense but continue to use 'adult education' to refer to the more academic side of community education or when dealing with the more traditional classes and courses.

3.   We have also felt it necessary to consider what the word 'adult' should be held to mean in the context of our remit. The age of political majority is 18 and the school leaving age is now 16. The number of pupils staying on at

school beyond the statutory leaving age is steadily increasing and many, in fact, are still at school when they reach their political majority. Many education authorities have already adopted 18 as the minimum qualifying age for enrolment in adult education classes. But they have not laid this down to the absolute exclusion of those under 18. We think it necessary to ensure that there is no gap between formal school provision and adult education provision and therefore to make our first recommendation to the effect that *'adult' for the purposes of Part II of this report, in which we develop our ideas for the future, should mean any person who has reached statutory school leaving age*.

4.   The expression 'voluntary leisure time courses' we have defined as meaning courses of instruction which have no specific vocational purpose and which are voluntarily attended by a student in the time when he is not engaged in his normal daily occupation. We have included within this definition however courses which are not specifically vocational and which are attended by students during periods of paid leave granted by employers for the purpose.

5.   In several parts of our report we use the terms 'initial education' and 'continuing education'. We take initial education to mean all the educational experiences undertaken by a person prior to the time he takes up his first full-time career post. On this basis it includes all school-based or compulsory education and also the education of those who go straight from school to a university or college in pursuit of higher qualifications. In addition we regard those whose immediate post-school employment involves vocational day-release or sandwich courses or apprenticeship training schemes as still undergoing initial education. All educational experiences which an individual undergoes subsequent to or additional to this initial education we term continuing education.

2 Historical Review

18TH AND 19TH CENTURIES

6.   The early development of adult education in Scotland took various forms. The 18th century saw the birth of a variety of literary and scientific societies which led ultimately to the formation of the Royal Society of Edinburgh in 1782. Agricultural societies, too, were founded in various parts of the country, often under the patronage of a local nobleman or laird. For example, one was founded in Ormiston, East Lothian, in 1736 for 'discussion of questions of rural economy and agricultural improvement'. Another, founded in Ettrick as 'a school where the young farmer will see the real and apparent properties of live-stock', might well be seen as the forerunner of the Young Farmers Clubs of today. Pioneering work was carried out in the provision of lectures and classes for artisans in Glasgow, work mainly associated with the names of Professor John Anderson and Professor George Birkbeck. The interest and benevolence of Anderson, who occupied the Chair of Natural Philosophy in the University of Glasgow from 1760 to 1796, led to the founding of the Andersonian Institute, later to become the Royal College of Science and Technology and now the University of Strathclyde. Birkbeck, who was

Professor of Natural Philosophy in the Institute from 1799 to 1804, organised popular lectures and classes of various kinds which evoked an enthusiastic response from artisans and established a pattern which was followed for long after his departure to London. A quite different form of development at this time is represented by the Corresponding Societies which reflected the growing political awareness of the latter part of the century and which were centres of discussion and debate.

7. In the early years of the 19th Century evening classes figured in Robert Owen's experiment at New Lanark, and in Edinburgh the School of Art was founded for working tradesmen and became, it is generally accepted, the model for the Mechanics Institutes which emerged to meet the economic and industrial changes by then affecting the country. The Edinburgh Philosophical Association was founded in 1835, to be copied elsewhere, and little more than a decade later came the establishment of the Glasgow Athenaeum, destined to follow a path in some ways not dissimilar to that taken by the Andersonian Institute and to become the Royal Scottish Academy of Music and Drama. In the middle years of the century, too, while in Edinburgh James Young Simpson, the pioneer of anaesthetics, gave what he called 'lectures to working classes', developments in provision for adults in Glasgow and the West of Scotland reflected in some degree the influence of new social and political movements such as Chartism and Trade Unionism. The University Extension Movement, founded in Cambridge by a Scottish professor, James Stuart, to encourage and enable the universities to contribute in a sustained way to the education of the mass of the population, soon spread to Scotland and all the Scottish universities participated in it for some years. In 1887 Patrick Geddes, a leader of the Extension Movement, organised the first international summer school in Europe when he brought together in Scotland men interested in both science and the liberal arts.

1900–1945

8. In 1901 the then Scotch Education Department issued a circular urging the introduction in continuation classes of 'courses which have no special relation to any particular occupation but rather concern the individual as a member of the social community'. This was the beginning of Government encouragement of non-vocational education of the kind with which this report is concerned.

9. Despite the significant part played by Scotsmen in early and important developments in adult education both in Scotland and elsewhere the inescapable fact is that Scotland was very much slower than England to develop adult education in an organised way. This may well have been due in part to the fact that young Scots traditionally enjoyed much greater opportunities to proceed to higher education, including university education, than their English counterparts, with the result that the demand for extra-mural education was correspondingly less. Whatever the reason, there has been throughout a difference in the pace of development and this is well illustrated by the early history of the Workers' Educational Association (hereinafter referred to as the WEA). The Association was founded in England in 1903 by Albert Mansbridge and quickly flourished, particularly in the industrial areas. It was not until almost 10 years later however that the Association made an effective start in

Scotland when tutorial classes in history were begun in Edinburgh, followed shortly afterwards by classes in Aberdeen. Almost immediately however the First World War broke out and development came to a halt.

10. The birth of the Labour movement had led to the provision of classes for trade unionists and to the founding in 1921 of the National Council of Labour Colleges which finally had its headquarters at Tillicoultry. These Colleges pioneered the provision of independent working class education and trained thousands of men and women to serve their fellows on committees, in local government and in Parliament. The success of the NCLC's varied programme of correspondence courses was probably the outstanding example of sustained educational effort affecting large numbers of working people.

11. The year 1919 saw the publication of the report of the Smith Committee, which, as we have already indicated, had been set up by the Ministry of Reconstruction to consider 'the provision for, and possibilities of, Adult Education (other than technical and vocational) and to make recommendations'. This report was followed in 1924 by the issue of Adult Education Regulations and together they provided a great incentive to expansion in England and Wales particularly through the creation of university extra-mural departments and the development of university extension. The Regulations, which did not apply to Scotland, provided for exchequer grant aid to universities and voluntary bodies active in adult education in England and Wales and accorded 'responsible body' status to those specifically approved for the purpose. This gave them statutory power to provide adult education, a power previously vested solely in the local education authorities. In Scotland however the position remained largely unchanged. Only limited provision of adult education was made, mainly by voluntary agencies and by the universities, of which the University of Glasgow set up an Extra-Mural Committee in 1924 and the University of Edinburgh in 1929. There was no major attempt to alter or improve the position generally. No steps were taken to provide exchequer grant aid to voluntary bodies in respect of adult education provision and no distinction was drawn between adult education classes provided by education authorities and other kinds of continuation or evening classes. The situation improved slightly in 1926 when, with the issue of the Continuation Class Code, adult education classes were distinguished, for the first time in regulations, from other kinds of continuation classes. The next significant change came in 1934 when the provisions relating to adult education were removed from the Continuation Class Code and the Adult Education (Scotland) Regulations 1934 were introduced. These removed from adult education some of the restrictions of the Code and empowered education authorities to co-operate with voluntary bodies in securing adult education provision within their areas. It was made quite clear however that the body financially and administratively responsible for the provision of courses under their terms was the education authority. The 1934 Regulations laid it down that courses arranged under them should be designed for the liberal education of persons over 18 years of age and so arranged as to give them opportunity for continuous progressive study. They stipulated that classes should fall into three main categories: (a) tutorial classes extending over at least two years and approximating to a university standard; (b) preparatory tutorial classes for students proposing to proceed to classes of the kind described in (a) who required some preliminary instruction; (c) other classes of a less specialised kind. They also dealt with the number and duration of meetings and the size of classes.

12. A notable innovation was soon to follow. The Marquess of Lothian had in 1933 offered his home, the historic Newbattle Abbey, for use in connection with the education of adults. With generous assistance from the Carnegie United Kingdom Trust towards the cost of its adaptation the Abbey was opened in 1937 as the first residential college of adult education in Scotland. In 1938 the Adult Education (Scotland) (Residential Institutions) Regulations were introduced. They provided for the payment of grants in aid of the costs of maintenance of approved residential institutions providing full-time instruction in liberal education for persons over 18 years of age and Newbattle Abbey was thus able to be given essential assistance. Again however further development was interrupted by a war. In 1939 the College was requisitioned and served a variety of uses before being returned to adult education in 1950.

THE EDUCATION (SCOTLAND) ACT 1945

13. Immediately after the war the far reaching Education (Scotland) Act 1945 came into operation. It developed the concept of an informal further education service for both young people and adults through provisions which:

(a) required education authorities 'to secure that adequate and efficient provision is made throughout their area of all forms of primary, secondary and further education';

(b) defined further education as including 'voluntary part-time and full-time courses of instruction for persons over school age' and 'voluntary leisure-time occupation, in such organised cultural training and recreative activities as are suited to their requirements, for persons over school age';

(c) required education authorities 'to secure that facilities for primary, secondary and further education provided for their area include adequate facilities for recreation and social and physical training'; and

(d) required education authorities, in discharging their duties with regard to recreation and social and physical training, to 'have regard to the expediency of co-operating with any voluntary societies or bodies whose objects include the provision of facilities or the organisation of activities of a similar character'.

14. In discharging their responsibilities under the 1945 Act the education authorities made some provision at their own hand and also entered into co-operative arrangements with other bodies concerned with particular aspects of the education of adults. Most prominent among these were the universities. The Scottish universities (then only four in number: Aberdeen, Edinburgh, Glasgow and St Andrews) were in a very different position as regards adult education from those in England and Wales. They had no tradition of deep involvement in university extension work, nor had they benefited from the exchequer assistance for the provision of adult education courses which the English universities had enjoyed since 1924. They had made provision of adult education throughout the years but it had been limited by financial constraints since they had to finance their courses out of their own resources, generally by charging economic fees. This was expensive for the student and risky for the university, which frequently suffered financial loss on courses that failed to enrol sufficient students. The post-war revival of interest in education at all levels which came in the wake of the 1945 Act

had some effect on provision for adults and helped to bring about closer co-operation between the education authorities and the universities.

15.   A further stimulus was provided by the 1952 Report on Further Education by the Advisory Council on Education in Scotland, which drew attention to the duty placed upon the education authorities to ensure the provision of adequate facilities and stated 'therefore, it is the merest common sense that any work in this field by the universities should be undertaken in co-operation with the education authorities and be regarded as part of the public system of further education. We see no reason why there should not be the most friendly relationship between the universities and the education authorities in their region, and we are confident that the universities will benefit by closer association with the general system of education'. The same report also paid tribute to the WEA 'for the valuable pioneering work they have done and are still doing'. At the same time it pointed out that 'the WEA have tended to regard the higher intellectual groups as their main sphere of influence' and that 'they have up till now catered for a very restricted clientele; and we suggest that the time has come for them to review their policy. If they are to undertake the promotion of liberal studies for all sections of the population they will have to cast the net more widely'. As a consequence of the Council's Report the education authorities, which had previously done little themselves in the way of adult education but had tended to rely on other agencies, began to become more directly involved. Extra-mural committees based on the four universities of that time were formed. The membership of these committees included representatives of the education authorities of the extra-mural provinces, the WEA, and other bodies active in the field of adult education. Their main purpose was to define and promote an enlarged university contribution to adult education, chiefly through a variety of courses reflecting established university disciplines. The extra-mural departments of the Universities of Glasgow and Edinburgh, which were set up on a permanent basis with the appointment of a full-time Director of Extra-Mural Studies in 1946 and 1949 respectively, played an important part in organising courses and promoting a growing awareness of the values attached to adult education. A further consequence of the Advisory Council Report was the extension of grant aid from the Scottish Education Department to voluntary organisations. In 1952 Regulations were introduced which permitted 'approved associations' to be assisted in respect of their administrative costs and which thus enabled the extra-mural committees and the WEA, both nationally and at district level, to apply for financial assistance.

16.   The period of the early 1960s marked a gradual awakening of public concern about the leisure-time education of adults. Much of the impetus and direction came from the extra-mural departments. Aberdeen and St Andrews had followed their sister universities, first in making part-time appointments of professional staff in 1956. Later in the same year Aberdeen made its first full-time appointment and St Andrews did likewise in 1963. The University of Dundee, on its separation from St Andrews, maintained the full-time appointment in order to sustain the continuity of development which was by then well-established North of the Tay. The presence in the growing extra-mural education departments of virtually the only professional adult educators in Scotland inevitably meant that much depended on the initiative which came from them. Fortunately there were others who gave ready support. The Scottish Institute of Adult Education, established in 1949 as a regular forum for dis-

cussion and information, attracted to senior office professional educationists of prominence who in a voluntary capacity expended much time and effort in winning public recognition of adult needs. The WEA Districts provided both voluntary and professional support. Newbattle Abbey College increased the number of places in its full-time course and was able to obtain the financial support of the local authorities and the Scottish Education Department on a scale which allowed a new residential block to be built and a major rehabilitation of the main building to be carried out. As significant as any other development was the initiative taken by two education authorities. In 1965 the Fife Authority initiated a system of full-time tutor organisers, each based on a further education college. At about the same time the Edinburgh Authority appointed several full-time principal tutors with area responsibilities.

YOUTH AND COMMUNITY SERVICE

17. The 1945 Act led also to the evolution of the youth and community service as a comprehensive service for young people and adults. Although voluntary bodies had been concerned with the promotion of social, cultural and recreative activities for very many years, it was the powers conferred on education authorities by the 1945 Act which gave some cohesion to the service. Until the 1960s however expansion continued to be slow, largely because of adverse economic conditions. Professional training for youth and community workers was introduced in 1946 under the auspices of the Scottish Youth Leadership Training Association but came to an end in 1950 and it was not until 1960 that such training was re-introduced. Since then training arrangements have expanded and the number of professionally trained workers has very greatly increased. In turn, this has led to steady development of the service, with the bulk of the activity in the youth sector but with a significant trend towards community work and the development of all-age community centres. This development was greatly aided by the introduction by the Secretary of State in 1961 of a scheme of capital grants under the Further Education (Scotland) Regulations 1959 to assist local voluntary youth organisations to acquire or improve premises and to equip them, provided the relevant education authority gave a grant of not less than half the Secretary of State's grant. A somewhat similar scheme was operated under the Physical Training and Recreation Act 1937 to assist local voluntary community organisations to provide or improve centres or halls used for social and recreational purposes. Grants under this latter scheme were not conditional on a local authority contribution, although many authorities did contribute. Most of the grants went to projects in rural areas. Under the 1937 Act, also, the Secretary of State made capital grants to local sports clubs to assist them to provide or improve their sports facilities. These three schemes of grants enabled voluntary bodies to take a much larger part in the provision and improvement of social, cultural and recreational facilities than would otherwise have been possible, but much the major part in providing facilities has been taken by education and other local authorities.

18. It has not been the practice to make grants from central Government funds to local voluntary organisations to assist their maintenance and running costs, such assistance being a matter for education authorities and local authorities. The Secretary of State however makes grants to the national

headquarters of about 40 youth and community organisations to assist their expenditure on administration and training and until 1971 offered similar grants to national sports organisations under the Physical Training and Recreation Act 1937. In 1972 responsibility for all sports grants, both local and national, was transferred to the Scottish Sports Council which receives an annual grant-in-aid from the Secretary of State. In 1973 the two schemes of capital grants to local voluntary youth and to local voluntary community organisations were combined into one scheme administered under the Further Education (Scotland) Regulations 1959 and the maximum grant was greatly increased.

19. The expansion of the youth and community service and its recognition as an important part of the education service as a whole has been greatly assisted by the work of the national body known as the Standing Consultative Council on Youth and Community Service which was established by the Secretary of State in 1963 as successor to the Standing Consultative Council on Youth Service. The Council is concerned with informal educational and leisure-time activities for young people and adults but is not directly concerned with the more formal type of activities normally understood by the term 'adult education'. It consists of nominees of the Secretary of State, the local authority associations, the Standing Conference of Voluntary Youth Organisations, the Scottish Council of Social Service, the Committee of Principals of Colleges of Education and professional associations concerned with education and youth and community work. The members are appointed by the Secretary of State and the Council is serviced by the Scottish Education Department. As a result of the Council's efforts significant advances have been made, particularly in building up the infra-structure of the service. The Council has advised on training for full-time and part-time youth and community workers, the establishment of an information service on youth and community matters, research projects, Government grants to local voluntary youth organisations for building projects, and a wide range of other subjects. It organises conferences, publishes newsletters and suggests new measures to education authorities and voluntary bodies. It has produced reports on a range of topics, the most important and influential of its more recent reports being 'Community of Interests'* published in 1968. This dealt with relationships in the field of community education and leisure, and with co-operation between schools, further education and statutory and voluntary bodies in the provision of leisure-time activities.

THE EDUCATION (SCOTLAND) ACT 1969

20. The concept of leisure-time education as including a wide range of activities of different degrees of formality was further expressed in the Education (Scotland) Act 1969 which widened the definition of further education in the 1945 Act (see paragraph 13) to include 'social, cultural and recreative activities and physical education and training, either as part of a course of instruction or as voluntary leisure-time occupation' and omitted the phrase 'for persons over school age'. It also empowered education authorities to secure for their area 'the provision of adequate facilities for social, cultural and recreative

*HMSO 35p.

activities and for physical education and training' for members of the general public whether or not they were following organised courses of school or further education.

3 Present Position

SCOTTISH INSTITUTE OF ADULT EDUCATION

21.   While there is a Standing Consultative Council on Youth and Community Service, there is no directly comparable national body charged with the development of adult education. In its absence, the Scottish Institute of Adult Education has sought to perform for adult education some of the functions which the Standing Consultative Council has performed for the youth and community service. The Institute which was established as the successor to the Scottish branch of the British Institute of Adult Education maintains close association with the National Institute of Adult Education (England and Wales). It is a voluntary association of organisations and individuals concerned with adult education, and includes representatives of the universities, the education authorities, the WEA, and other voluntary and public bodies interested in the development of studies among adults. It has encouraged experiments and new techniques in adult education, has maintained links with similar organisations in other countries, and, through its conferences and publications, has kept the values of adult education before the public. Its resources are however limited and its income, consisting almost entirely of grants from the education authorities and the Scottish Education Department, is barely sufficient to maintain a small headquarters office, a full-time secretary and clerical support. Its work is largely dependent on the voluntary efforts of individual representatives of its member bodies. Despite its very limited resources the Institute has done much to promote adult education in Scotland and has pressed the needs of adult education on the education authorities and the Scottish Education Department. Its working parties have sought to formulate policy and its annual conferences have been a forum for the discussion of policy matters. Its reports, newsletters and yearbook have helped to keep adult educators in Scotland in touch with new ideas and with new developments in the United Kingdom and elsewhere.

22.   Since its formation, the Institute has sought in various ways to persuade the Government and the education authorities that the educational and social importance of adult education justifies the allocation of much greater public resources to it. In 1965 in discussions with the Scottish Education Department the Institute indicated that its area of interest in the further education of adults could be described as 'Formal and informal cultural activities, aesthetic as well as intellectual, requiring participation, both for the development of the individual and for active citizenship under changing conditions'. Following these discussions the Institute appointed a working party to consider the finance of adult education in Scotland, and the working party's report, which dealt with administration, physical provision and research as well as with

finance, was published by the Institute in 1968.* The report did not recommend any significant change in the organisation of adult education or in the respective responsibilities of the Scottish Education Department and the education authorities for financing it, but urged that much greater support should be made available from public funds, both from the education authorities and from the Government, for adult education activities, adult centres and short-term residential accommodation. It also drew attention to social changes affecting adult education, to likely future developments, to specific difficulties and anomalies in the financing and administration of adult education in Scotland and to the overlapping interests of the statutory and other bodies concerned. We have found this report of great value in considering our own remit.

WORKERS' EDUCATIONAL ASSOCIATION

23.   While many voluntary organisations, particularly those in the youth and community service, are concerned in varying degrees with informal education in the broadest social sense and some have made a substantial contribution to the education of adults as well as of young people, the national voluntary body most directly involved in adult education in the more traditional sense has undoubtedly been the WEA. Although its activities in Scotland are relatively less extensive than elsewhere in the United Kingdom, it has in Scotland over 30 branches with about 1,300 individual members. It is organised in three districts, each of which is in receipt of grant from the Scottish Education Department towards administrative and organising costs under the Further Education (Scotland) Regulations 1959. These grants are subject to conditions similar to those attached to grants given to national voluntary youth and community organisations. They cannot be used for local expenditure such as the provision of classes and the payment of teachers and lecturers, grants for such purposes being a matter for the education authorities. The WEA promotes adult education generally, organises classes and co-operates with education authorities in providing classes.

24.   In 1968 the WEA in Scotland sought from the Secretary of State 'providing powers' similar to those which 'responsible bodies' (the WEA, university extra-mural departments and certain other bodies) already had in England and Wales. Under the English arrangements the responsible bodies receive grant from the Department of Education and Science towards the cost of employing tutors and providing classes, and classes are thus provided both by the local education authorities and by the responsible bodies. The Scottish WEA considered:

(a)   that the existing adult education arrangements did not meet the needs of educationally under-privileged adults and that the type of classes provided were unsuitable for many of them; and

(b)   that the Secretary of State should make grants to the Scottish WEA districts of 90 per cent of their expenditure on the provision of classes and the employment of staff and 75 per cent of their administrative expenditure.

We understand that, broadly speaking, this still represents the WEA view.

*Scottish Adult Education—Report of the Working Party on Adult Education in Scotland—25p.

EXTRA-MURAL COMMITTEES AND DEPARTMENTS

25. A substantial proportion of courses with a pronounced intellectual content related to or derived from the various established academic disciplines are provided through the agency of the university extra-mural departments. In accordance with the policy already described the extra-mural departments do not receive grant aid from the Scottish Education Department for the provision of courses in the areas which they serve, Government assistance being given only towards administrative and organising costs. This is not however given direct to the universities, but to the Extra-Mural Education Committees based on the Universities of Glasgow, Aberdeen, Edinburgh and Dundee and serviced by the extra-mural departments of these universities. These committees all include representatives of the appropriate universities, the education authorities of the area and the WEA and are approved by the Secretary of State 'as voluntary associations', thus making them eligible for grant under the Further Education (Scotland) Regulations 1959. No Government grant is given for the employment of tutors or the provision of accommodation, support for those purposes being a matter for the member education authorities. The several committees are financed by their member authorities in different ways. Those in membership of the Glasgow Extra-Mural Committee make contributions on an agreed basis towards the expenses of the Committee which then organises the classes, employs the tutors and pays their fees on a uniform scale. The administrative work is carried out by the Extra-Mural Department of the University of Glasgow. The Extra-Mural Departments of the Universities of Aberdeen, Dundee and Edinburgh also organise classes on behalf of their committees but the member education authorities themselves pay fees direct to tutors and on a variety of scales.

26. The University of St Andrews appointed a Director of Extra-Mural Studies in 1967. Subsequently, a Consultative Committee for Extra-Mural Education representing the University and Fife and Clackmannan Education Authorities was set up, but there is no extra-mural education committee analogous to those referred to above and the Scottish Education Department does not make a grant towards the administrative expenses of the Consultative Committee. Nor does the Department make any grants in respect of extra-mural activities undertaken by other Scottish universities.

RESIDENTIAL CENTRES

27. We have already mentioned Newbattle Abbey College, which is still the only long-term residential adult education college in Scotland, but its main courses are not directly relevant to the subject of our remit since they are full-time and, apart from being residential, are analogous to certain full-time courses in colleges of further education. In 1973 the College introduced a 2-year Diploma Course intended primarily for mature students wishing to proceed to University or other institution of higher education. The Diploma has been accepted by the Scottish Universities Council on Entrance for purposes of admission to a Scottish university, subject to the appropriate faculty requirements. The College is managed by a Board of Governors widely representative of adult educational and other interests and receives an annual

grant from the Scottish Education Department. The development of short-term residential provision was also much slower and much later in Scotland than in England, although Newbattle Abbey College has for long been used for short-term courses when the main courses are not in session. During the 1960s however residential centres were opened at Middleton Hall and Carberry Tower in Midlothian and at Scottish Churches' House, Dunblane, although they were not intended specifically for general adult education use. A number of education authorities, recognising the value of residential facilities for the in-service training of teachers and the training of part-time youth and community workers, acquired various properties and adapted them to a high standard of suitability for these purposes. There was also a substantial increase in the number of modern university and other student residences able to provide accommodation for short-term courses during vacations. The availability of these centres and residences has encouraged the provision of week-end schools of many kinds and has facilitated the establishment of residential courses for working adults. Consequently, the growth in the number of summer schools has been such that their organisation is now a significant part of the work of some adult education agencies.

OVERLAPPING OF FORMAL AND INFORMAL

28.   In the foregoing paragraphs we have sought to summarise the development of adult education and the work of the main organisations concerned with it or with other leisure-time activities for adults in the educational field. Certain aspects of the work of a number of the organisations in the latter category, eg the Townswomen's Guilds, the Women's Rural Institutes, the Young Men's and Young Women's Christian Associations and the Churches do not appear to differ greatly in kind or principle from some of the work of the more specifically adult education bodies, however much their stated objectives and educational approach may differ. This overlapping of what might be described as the more formal and the more informal approaches to the leisure-time education of adults is also apparent when we consider the activities of the education authorities themselves.

EDUCATION AUTHORITIES

29.   As will be seen from Appendix III, which we consider in detail later, the great majority of leisure-time adult education students attend classes organised by the education authorities. Under the Education (Scotland) Acts sole statutory responsibility for adult education continues to rest with the 35 County and City education authorities who have a duty to secure throughout their areas adequate and efficient provision for voluntary classes and courses. They may discharge their responsibilities in co-operation with other agencies, in the manner we have already described, and they may assist these agencies with grants or by making accommodation, lecturers and other services available to them, either free or at reduced cost; but the majority of adult education classes they provide at their own hand. Under the Local Government (Scotland) Act 1973 responsibilities for provision under the Education (Scotland) Acts will be taken over by 9 regional and 3 islands authorities from 15 May 1975, but the duties and powers of the new education authorities will be substantially the same as those of the present ones.

30.   In almost all education authority areas adult education is dealt with by a further education sub-committee which is frequently also concerned with the youth and community service, the youth employment services and, in county council areas, public libraries (after 1975 public libraries will be a district and island responsibility except in the 3 most thinly populated regions where they will be a regional responsibility). The staff responsible for the administration of adult education are usually headed by a Depute or Assistant Director of Education whose duties normally extend also to the youth and community service. We discuss the general staffing position later in this report, but here it can confidently be stated that the total number of staff at present responsible solely for adult education is small. Edinburgh Education Authority has 5 principal tutors with area responsibilities each directly answerable to an Assistant Director of Education. Fife has 4 full-time tutor organisers normally attached to the staff of a College of Further Education; their areas are the same as the catchment areas of the Colleges to which they are attached and they operate in co-operation with the Extra-Mural Department of the University of Edinburgh and the South-East Scotland District of the WEA. These developments have not been followed in other areas.

31.   The greater part of education authority provision for adults is made in what are variously called evening institutes, adult centres or further education centres; most are housed in schools. In the majority of cases they cater both for vocationally directed courses and for other courses but there is an increasing trend to transfer vocationally directed courses, including courses leading to the Scottish Certificate of Education, to colleges of further education. Where both types of course are provided in the same centre the vocationally directed courses usually start earlier in the year. Evening institutes, even including some with over 1,000 students, are run by part-time heads who are usually day-school teachers. A substantial number of leisure-time classes are also provided under the auspices of the youth and community service, both in community centres and in schools. The organisation of classes provided in this way becomes the responsibility of full-time youth and community workers, with the result that education authorities feel less need for full-time personnel devoted entirely to adult education.

32.   There appears to be very little difference between many of the leisure-time courses and classes provided by the education authorities through the youth and community service and those provided by the same authorities through their further education or adult education machinery. At one time it might have been reasonable to say that leisure-time courses provided through further education or adult education were more structured, more formal and possibly more rigorous, but this is no longer true as a general proposition. Nevertheless in some areas artificial barriers appear to have been created between the two kinds of provision by the same education authority, and in others there is a certain amount of duplication. For example, it is possible for two separate classes in the same subject, catering for broadly the same kind of students, to be held in the same building and taught by the same teacher, one as a youth and community class and the other as an adult education class, and for the teacher concerned to receive two different rates of pay.

33.   In the development of leisure-time classes under the auspices of the youth and community service building programmes have been a significant

factor. Over the period 1966–72, approximately £7½m was spent by education authorities on the provision and improvement of social, cultural and recreational buildings which they themselves managed and on grant aid to voluntary bodies undertaking similar projects. Nearly two-thirds of this expenditure was for community centres and village halls and about one-third for community provision linked to schools. These community buildings, designed and furnished to encourage informality, provide a very suitable setting for many kinds of adult education activities and tend to attract people to whom the more formal setting of an educational institution seems rather forbidding.

PROVISION AND PARTICIPANTS

34.   Appendix III indicates that of the total of 217,000 enrolments in adult education classes in 1972/73 about 189,000 were in classes organised directly by the education authorities, about 21,000 in classes organised by the University Extra-Mural Education Committees, over 4,500 in classes organised by the WEA and 2,200 in classes organised by the central institutions (which are directly financed by the Scottish Education Department). Of the enrolments in education authority classes however about 98,000, slightly more than half, were in physical education and handicraft and hobby classes and about 51,000, almost entirely of women, were in cookery and needlework classes. The remaining 40,000 were in a wide variety of classes covering broadly the same range of subjects as the classes organised by extra-mural education committees and by the WEA. It is noticeable however that a higher proportion of extra-mural education committee students were in classes of the more cultural and academic kind including particularly history, science, social studies and the visual arts. The classes in the central institutions were almost entirely concerned with music, handicraft, drama and visual arts.

35.   The figures in Appendix III relate to enrolments and an individual student may enrol in more than one class and in more than one centre. Moreover there is some reason to believe that enrolments recorded by the WEA in classes organised by them may also be recorded separately by the education authority actually providing the classes. Thus the total number of students is probably significantly less than the number of enrolments and, as the effective attendance figures show, there is a considerable falling off in attendances in the course of the session. It is clear that the proportion of adults affected by the existing provision of leisure-time courses is not more than 4 per cent of the total adult population. The range of subjects offered is wide but the great weight of interest is in hobbies, physical activities and domestic skills. The numbers in classes in science, social affairs and cultural subjects are much less. Little is offered in other areas of personal concern such as community and environmental problems, family budgeting, parenthood, consumer education and family health. While therefore the present position gives cause for modest satisfaction in some respects, there is good reason for considerable dissatisfaction in others.

36.   In order to secure more detailed information about the kind of students taking part in leisure-time classes and about their interests and attitudes, we arranged three case studies with the co-operation of the education authorities and the university extra-mural departments of the areas concerned. The areas chosen were : Argyll, a rural area ; Dundee, an industrial area ; and

Fife, a mixed rural and industrial area. A total of over 1,600 questionnaires were issued and nearly 1,200 were returned. (A summary of the findings is contained in Appendix XIII). While the numbers were too small to enable firm conclusions to be drawn, the results of the studies provided some confirmation of impressions gained from other sources. The following points emerged:

(a)   more than two-thirds of the students were women;

(b)   only about 15 per cent of the students were aged under 25 while more than 25 per cent were aged over 55;

(c)   the occupations of the students indicated that over 80 per cent were in the top three classes of the Registrar General's socio-economic scale, ie the students were mainly middle class; less than 10 per cent were members of a trade union whereas nearly 20 per cent were members of a professional association;

(d)   the formal educational qualifications of the students were substantially higher than the national average, nearly one quarter of them having university degrees or other higher educational qualifications;

(e)   many students regularly attended classes from one year to another and were satisfied with the standard of classes, their duration and the quality of the tuition provided.

Limited as they were, the case studies tended to confirm the widely held view that an unduly high proportion of those to whom adult education courses offer a satisfactory leisure-time activity are the older, the better-educated and the more affluent. Those to whom adult education should be of most value are least involved.

THE NON-PARTICIPANTS

37.   It should be emphasised that the case studies, while providing some evidence about the students actually participating in adult education, told us nothing about the attitudes of the great majority of adults who do not attend, and never have attended, any classes or courses. It is to the interests of this great majority that the future development of adult education must in our view be directed. We were particularly disturbed at the low proportion of trade union members among the students involved in these case studies. Almost from the start of the adult education movement attention was paid to the problems of trade unionism and of industrial relations. This was a natural outcome of the emphasis given by the pioneers of adult education to the part it could play in meeting the educational needs of working people and helping them to improve their collective social and economic position. Although the provision of education for trade unionists has expanded considerably as a result of the efforts of the WEA, the university extra-mural departments, colleges of commerce, the National Council of Labour Colleges and the trades unions themselves through the Trades Union Congress Education Service and other agencies, it clearly still falls far short of the need. There are however a number of fields in which there are extensive arrangements for providing adults with voluntary leisure-time courses directed to specific purposes which are not normally regarded as part of adult education. Courses for members of Children's Panels established under the Social Work (Scotland) Act and courses for voluntary leaders and workers in youth and community organisations are examples of these. Such courses are not included in the

figures given in Appendix III, but in our view they can properly be regarded as part of adult education and they affect a substantial number of adults.

38. It is clear however that the vast majority of adults in Scotland take no part in leisure-time courses and show no desire to do so. Despite the devoted efforts of many adult educators over the years what has so far been achieved for the education of adults falls far short of what in our view could reasonably be expected and the service has so far failed to make itself attractive to the bulk of the adult population despite the current widespread concern with educational problems. The absence of an established career pattern and the extremely limited number of posts in adult education have provided little incentive for anyone to enter the service full-time. This reflects the low priority accorded to adult education by both local and central government. More fundamentally however it reflects what we consider to be the most serious weakness—the absence of a comprehensive view of the nature and function of adult education in our society.

4 Statistics

SCOTTISH EDUCATIONAL STATISTICS

39. The Committee have experienced a good deal of difficulty in assessing the present position of adult education and in formulating proposals for the future because of the lack of adequate statistical information relating to non-vocational adult education. The annually published volume 'Scottish Educational Statistics'*, provides comprehensive information about most aspects of education in Scotland but we were disappointed to find how little information it contained specifically about adult education. It includes two tables (Nos 33 and 34 in the 1972 edition) which provide: (a) a classification of the courses provided by education authorities, by central institutions and by extra-mural departments and the WEA; (b) the numbers of students, distinguishing males from females, enrolling for and the numbers making at least two thirds of the possible attendances at courses of various duration in the subject categories identified; (c) the percentage of effective students to numbers enrolled—classified by sex and by providing agencies; and (d) comparative figures for the four previous years. Useful though this information is, much more is required. For example:

(a) *Staffing* There is a need for statistics giving the numbers of administrators and of teachers, distinguishing between full-time and part-time staff and providing information on their professional qualifications.

(b) *Students* The statistics at present furnished on student numbers are based on information which takes no account of the fact that many students attend more than one course during the session. Because of this the figures for enrolments exceed the actual number of individuals who participate in adult education. There is perhaps no wholly acceptable and satisfactory way of completely avoiding this, but, if all the agencies providing adult education were to include a question on their enrolment form regarding the extent to which each student is involved in other courses, this could provide

*(HMSO).

16

a better basis than is now available for estimating the extent to which figures for enrolments exceed the number of individual students. In addition, statistics of enrolments should be gathered and presented in such a way as to give information on the age as well as the sex of students. Information should also be provided about students attending short-term residential courses and students taking correspondence courses.

(c) *Finance* 'Scottish Educational Statistics' throws little light on the finances of adult education. Obviously there are great difficulties in calculating at all accurately the total expenditure by an education authority on the provision of adult education. Even if financial information were confined to recurrent costs and excluded the cost of buildings and other capital items, few of which are used exclusively for adult education, the same difficulty would occur. The allocation of expenditure on staff, from the Director of Education to the school janitors, between adult education and the other branches of education could only be estimated and in many cases it would be wasteful to attempt such an allocation. However, improvements could and certainly should be made on the present practice under which even the salaries and fees paid to teachers are presented without distinguishing those which relate to adult education. Statistics on the income derived from fees should be presented alongside the other financial information; and it would be helpful if information could be assembled on expenditure incurred in providing for individuals and groups whose needs have been identified for special attention. More refined financial statistics are essential if the allocation of resources is to take proper account of policy objectives.

CASE STUDIES AND ENQUIRIES

40. It was because of the lack of adequate statistical information that we asked the Extra-Mural Departments of the Universities of Edinburgh, Glasgow and Dundee and the education authorities of Argyll, Dundee and Fife to carry out the case studies referred to in paragraph 36. In another attempt to secure more detailed information we addressed special enquiries to education authorities and others and all were extremely helpful in providing us with such of the required information as they could. In practice however most education authorities maintain only such statistics as they normally return to the Scottish Education Department and such additional information as they were able to give us was based largely on estimates (see Appendix XII).

GENERAL HOUSEHOLD SURVEY

41. We were particularly concerned about the absence of information about those who do not participate in adult education and the reasons for their non-participation. On the suggestion of the Committee, the Scottish Education Department and the Department of Education and Science have co-operated in making arrangements for questions on these matters to be included as from 1974 in the General Household Survey which is carried out on a United Kingdom basis. The questions are designed to ascertain, for example, whether non-participation is due to a lack of interest, lack of suitable provision, lack of opportunity for whatever reason or lack of information about the opportunities available.

CONCLUSION

42. Those responsible for the development of the adult service must be able to plan on the basis of fuller information than is currently available about the provision of adult education services and the use made of them. The importance of effective arrangements for the collection and collation of such statistics cannot be over-emphasised. The question of the collection and use of statistics is one of vital importance which requires much more attention that we have been able to give it. *We therefore recommend that the new council, which we later propose should be established, should examine the matter in detail and determine what statistics are required for the development of an efficient service such as we envisage.*

PART II

5 The Determinants of Change

43.   Adult education is part of the total educational system and is influenced by broadly the same factors as influence the rest of educational provision. In addition the character of school education has a considerable influence on all post-school education as regards both the foundations on which it has to build and the gaps it may have to fill.

44.   Education, although an agent of social change, is very much affected by other elements in society the most powerful of which are perhaps technology, economic development and social structure. Each of these elements interacts on the others as well as on the educational system itself. A comparison of the patterns of educational provision over the past century indicates the strong influences which social and technological change exert on educational provision. Increasing national wealth makes the expansion of educational provision possible. The content of education reacts to changes in technology despite the fact that the immediate aims of the educational system are not specifically vocational. For example, there are responses to changing social customs, illustrated by adjustments in the curricula for girls as a direct result of a change of attitude to the place of women in society. In addition, the increasing depth to which mathematics is now taught is a clear reflection of the increasing importance of measurement and quantification in industrial and commercial life. Many of the advances in knowledge which have contributed to the changes in educational content are in part a response to the new demands of technology.

45.   It is too limiting a view however to see education as simply responding to social needs as if it were merely a servant of society. The educational system is itself a main agent of change inasmuch as it affects the character of social and technical change, the pace at which new knowledge and attitudes are diffused throughout society and the quality of life in the broadest possible sense. The social position of clerical workers, for example, was earlier based

on the fact that a large proportion of the population could not read or write adequately. It has been substantially altered by the much more widespread and much higher standards of literacy which a century of compulsory education has produced. In a rather different way an education system can instil in young people a set of values and prejudices about different skills (eg intellectual as opposed to practical) which can ultimately have an effect on the value society attaches to particular types of employment. With education both influencing and being influenced by social factors it is clear that there can be no simple cause-and-effect relationship between education, technology and economic and social factors. Each change in any one factor may be both a response to changes in the others and a causal factor bringing about further changes.

46.   We therefore have a complex of changes which affect and are affected by the type and quality of educational provision. The changes are not always smooth and free from conflict. Particularly where social and moral values are involved educationists, especially those directly concerned with schools and the youth service, may find that the attitudes which young people absorb in their homes, at work, from their friends and in their social groups may conflict with those to which the educationists subscribe and which they seek to promote. It is in this difficult area of values, more than in any other area, that educationists must be prepared not merely to respond to the explicit demands placed on them by society as it now exists but also to help to change society in directions which are indicated by the values inherent in the educational process itself, ie those which lead to the extension of knowledge and its rational application to personal and community decisions. The effectiveness of education depends upon the ability of those responsible for providing it to detect, and even to foresee, significant social trends and by adapting their educational practice to use the opportunities that arise for the benefit of society and its individual members. It is therefore worthwhile setting out the major influences which can require changes in the provision for adult education, recognising that although these are enumerated separately they interact in the ways already described.

TECHNOLOGICAL CHANGE

47.   Technological change influences educational needs in three main ways: (a) by requiring new skills for use in conjunction with the new productive processes, (b) by requiring new skills to use the products which result from the application of new technologies and (c) by creating, as a result of the application of these new technologies, changed circumstances and problems with which individuals and societies must cope. Education for the use of new technologies in productive processes is primarily but not exclusively the concern of vocational education; and later in this report (para 79) we illustrate how the acquisition and use of consumer goods which are the end-product of the new technology play their part in creating new educational needs among adults. Perhaps even more important however are the other influences, less specific and distinct, exerted by technological change.

48.   Advances in medicine and pharmacology are the main cause of the need for greatly expanded educational provision for the elderly. The serious environmental problems created by technological change also create educational needs; for example education on accident prevention in the home,

on the use of garden pesticides, on environmental conservation and on planning procedures. The impact of technological change on employment opportunities is well recognised and this too gives rise to educational needs not all of which are narrowly vocational. Work is becoming so highly specialised and so subject to frequent innovation that those engaged in it must be able to mobilise knowledge with speed and to react quickly to new demands. Moreover the occupational mobility which is a feature of this development is accompanied by a social mobility which exerts its own particular pressures.

49. Technological changes affecting the media of communication and of entertainment are of especial importance, changing as they do the levels and patterns of both the demand for and the supply of education for adults. Radio and television are the most obvious and important examples but the great significance of the paperback revolution in publishing must also be recognised. Early fears of adult educationists that television would curtail the demand for traditional classes have not been borne out. In fact there has been an increase in the numbers and quality of students which to some extent at least is explained by the enlivening and stimulating effect which television programmes on such subjects as literature, art, current affairs, history and biology have had on a wide range of people who were previously unaware of the enjoyment which such intellectual activity can bring.

SOCIAL CHANGE

50. The social factors which generate new educational needs are very extensive and cannot be separated from more narrowly defined economic factors. The most fundamental social change is a demographic one. Already it is possible to detect that the pattern of demand for adult education has been affected by changes in the geographical location, age distribution and social mobility of the population. We comment in paragraph 75 on the increasing proportion of the adult population who are elderly.

51. All age groups are exposed to the pressures of change but they respond differently, in terms of values as well as of knowledge and skills. As a result a gap often exists between the young on the one hand and the middle-aged and elderly on the other. How far and in what direction efforts should be made to narrow this gap is a matter of some dispute but the dangers to social and family cohesion if it is allowed to widen are all too clear. This is a sphere in which adult education has an important contribution to make. It seems to us essential to recognise that the purpose of youth education is very similar to that of adult education and that any separation of the two is something to be avoided. In addition to this youth/age gap however social cohesion is further weakened by the increasing specialisation which results from technological and educational influences. One manifestation of this is the phenomenon of the 'two cultures'; the growing dependence of both citizens and public representatives on technical expertise is another. While there may be no complete answer to such problems the key importance of adult education as a means of reducing divergencies in approach and understanding should be obvious.

52. As a result not only of the complexity of the society in which they live but also of the specialised nature of the work they do and the difficulty of

relating it to the work of others, many people find it hard to comprehend certain features of modern life, even those features which closely affect them personally. The individual's sense of responsibility for his community and his willingness to take part in its collective activities and decisions tend to be reduced by his difficulty in seeing his own activities as related to those of the community or the country as a whole. Even if adult education may not be able fundamentally to alter individual selfishness with regard to social duties it can nevertheless develop a greater awareness of the extent to which the various elements of our complex society are interrelated.

53.   While it is true that many people are finding it more difficult to understand their place and their responsibilities in society, it is equally true that there is an increase in organised expression of concern about particular aspects of our society. It seems reasonable to interpret this increase in organised social caring as an effort by various groups to compensate for a decline in individual and family responsibility. The reassuring aspect of this apparent paradox of course is that social responsibilities are still recognised and undertaken though not always by the individuals from whom earlier generations would have expected the response.

54.   Also relevant to the role of adult education is the increasing desire on the part of the public to participate in the making of decisions. This desire is no less real for being expressed in a situation of general apathy. The apathy reflects the individual's feeling of powerlessness in a society that is intricate and remotely governed; the desire to participate reflects the democratic urge of a minority whose numbers are steadily growing. Whether one concentrates upon this minority or upon the currently apathetic majority it is impossible to escape the conviction that a democratic society, if it is to function effectively, must have an educated and well-informed electorate. In particular there must be a good supply of competent people willing to accept the responsibility of leadership at all levels and in many branches of life. Democracy cannot be taken for granted; it has been put under stress by the pressures of change and the problems of complex societies. A strong, broadly-based and highly professional system of education for adults is one of the best guarantees of a healthy democracy. This requires however that those providing the education should themselves respect the democratic rights of individuals and of sectional groups in society; and this in turn can best be ensured by encouraging some variety and indeed competition in the means of provision. The contribution which adult education can make to the development of a healthy and lively democracy requires that the organisation and character of educational provision be fully responsive to democratic influences.

55.   The rapid changes in the pattern of employment resulting from technological change bring about important changes in social structure, blurring or eliminating long-established distinctions of status and introducing new hierarchies within occupations, industry and society. Such changes in the pattern of demand for labour can create substantial and often localised unemployment and at the same time provide new opportunities for those who by their skills and their attitudes to change are capable of taking advantage of these opportunities. One change can lead to the need for further changes and have widespread and significant impact on individuals and groups, bringing strains and difficulties and sometimes creating individual or social neurosis.

56. But perhaps most important is education about change itself and about the need for individuals to adjust to change. A society can influence the attitude of its members to change in two important ways. The first is by providing material protection to shield the individual from the harshest consequences of changing circumstances. The second, in which education has a major role to play, is by helping the individual to understand the process of change—its causes, characteristics and consequences. By a better understanding of the process individuals and groups will be more able to take part in decisions about how the pace and character of change should be influenced so as to strike the balance between costs and benefits most acceptable to those affected. Only when both approaches, of protecting and informing, are adopted will the fear and resentment of change be minimised and smoother adjustment to change made possible.

57. The growth of leisure opens out exciting possibilities for expanding both the quantity and quality of adult education. Some very highly qualified specialists in the arts and the sciences, themselves enjoying more leisure, are showing an interest in communicating directly with the general public and in helping in the up-grading of the skills of less experienced and less well-qualified people. We believe that once the providing authorities express a clear intention to expand community education services the volume of help which could be obtained from such highly qualified specialists would be very great indeed. The voluntary organisations could play an important part in tapping this source of talent, since it is through the voluntary organisations that many of these professional people choose to make their contribution to social and community affairs.

EDUCATIONAL CHANGE

58. We come now to changes in educational theory and practice which are in part responses to the economic, technological and social factors mentioned and yet contribute to the very formation of these factors. The first is the erosion of the assumption that education is a once for all experience which happens to people for a prescribed period of time during their childhood and adolescence and that this is sufficient to equip them with all the knowledge, techniques and skills needed for a full life. There is a growing awareness that education should be a continuing experience spread over the whole of life. This is manifested in the importance now ascribed to pre-school education, in the ending of selection on entry to secondary education, in the growing attention in schools to guidance and leisure-time activities, in the provision of link courses between schools and further education establishments, in the expansion of vocational training and retraining and in the remarkable impact of the Open University.

59. The second change is that education now has a much broader connotation than formerly. No longer is it seen as being concerned solely or primarily with the training of the intellect. The aim is to enable each person to develop his various capacities to the full and to become an informed and responsible citizen. In schools this aim is pursued by ensuring that pupils participate in a wide range of activities—cultural, social, practical and recreational as well as intellectual. At the same time there has been a transfer of emphasis from

teaching to learning. Too often in the past the individual was treated as the passive object of the educational process; more and more he is being expected to control that process. This move towards individualised learning has been facilitated by educational technology in the form of broadcasting, programmed learning, language laboratories, data retrieval systems and so on. The significance of this trend is that education need no longer be treated as co-terminous with school, college or university. The mainspring of the educational process is the desire of people to learn whether at home, at work, in their leisure, in an educational institution or in a neighbourhood group.

60. Finally we wish to draw attention to a trend which follows from the others. The form and content of initial education is undergoing change. Instead of being concentrated on subject or content, attention is now being paid to the satisfaction of needs. Instead of being concentrated on what educational programmes contain, the emphasis is changing to what educational programmes do. There has been a steady move away from knowledge and skills which have an immediate, if limited, relevance to specific practical activities towards knowledge and skills which will enable the individual to perform a wide range of functions and to adjust to the many changes likely to confront him during his lifetime. Initial education now attaches greater importance than before to such key skills as problem-solving, decision-making, creativity, communication and leadership. As a consequence of these changes there has been a widening gap between the experience and understanding of parents regarding the nature and purpose of education and the experience of children. As more of the children whose school experience reflects these new approaches become adults this gap will narrow, and this should help to make the concept of life-long education more of a reality.

61. These are trends affecting the very basis of education. Their consequences are long-term and will be felt increasingly at all stages. Additionally, however, adult education is affected by developments in other parts of the educational field. With an increasing tendency for children to stay longer at school and with the minimum school leaving age now at 16, the general level of educational attainment of the school leaver is steadily being raised, providing a firmer foundation on which to build post-school education of all kinds. The school system is becoming more geared to producing questioning people of independent mind, conscious of their own capacity for development, and over the years it has been people with just these qualities who have become the main source of supply of adult education students. Thus the numbers and critical awareness of adults seeking post-school education can be expected to increase. In addition it seems certain that in future the school system will provide many more young people qualified to enter higher education than ever before. Not all will actually do so; some will lack the desire. But the number wishing to proceed to higher education seems likely to be so great that some sectors of the system of higher education may be forced to become even more selective than at present. In such an event the demand from highly qualified school leavers may operate to the particular detriment of the mature adult seeking a 'second chance' who could find this difficult enough to secure even if higher education were not constrained by lack of resources. This possibility should, as far as possible, be avoided since the high quality of 'second chance' students is universally acclaimed by those who teach them. Relevant alternative ways of obtaining post-school education will have to be made available.

62.   There will be difficulty in forecasting with precision the pattern of future demand for adult education because of the interaction of the several determinants and because much will depend on the individual's own interpretation of his needs and his reaction to the opportunities available to him. Forward thinking is essential but it has to be combined with flexibility if changing adult needs are to be met. The purpose of this review of the determinants of change in adult education has been to provide a framework within which the process of change to date and the need for changes in the future might be assessed.

6 Aims of Adult Education

GENERAL CONSIDERATIONS

63.   If the concept of education as a life-long process is to be given reality the education of adults must be accepted as an essential component of national policy designed to deal with the pressures of change and to improve the quality of life. The view of adult education as a marginal enterprise serving the interests of a relatively small proportion of the population can no longer be justified.

64.   Learning is a basic characteristic of life and man can learn as a result of every experience he undergoes. Education is a more organised or structured form of learning, by no means always associated with an institution. Continuing education, of which adult education is a part, is thus a series of learning experiences organised, structured or deliberately created by the learner or by others. It therefore covers a wide range of situations such as some forms of industrial and vocational training and retraining, the voluntary continuation of studies begun in initial education, activities undertaken for recreational purposes, the pursuit of knowledge and skills to further the aims of specific organisations, and individual study. The impact of newspapers and the broadcasting media or the activities of pressure groups and propaganda cannot be overlooked. Often the form of continuing education is highly specific to particular groups as in the case of sports clubs and political organisations. The educational service for adults must take account of other available educational opportunities and make provision which, taken together with these other opportunities, is comprehensive and relevant and is responsive to the needs not only of individuals but of the community and of society itself.

65.   Distinctions between different aspects or fields of education are necessary for administrative purposes but it has to be recognised that they are often imprecise and arbitrary. Adult education for example merges imperceptibly with formal education in schools, colleges and universities and with the informal activities of youth clubs, community centres and voluntary organisations. Distinctions made for administrative purposes can create barriers which impede the development of education as a life-long process. Various recent developments in initial education are removing traditional barriers and should help to foster a more widespread recognition of the continuity of education.

66.   With the very wide connotation given to education the question of values assumes greater importance. So long as education was equated with teaching

and restricted to specific institutions the aims and objectives of the process, though much argued over in detail, tended to be fairly uniform and to reflect the dominant values of the society which controlled it. Society is now less certain about the values it should uphold and tolerates a wide range. Individual freedom to question the value of established practices and institutions and to propose new forms is part of our democratic heritage. To maintain this freedom, resources should not be put at the disposal only of those who conform but ought reasonably to be made available to all for explicit educational purposes. The motives of those who provide education need not necessarily be identified with the motives of those for whom it is provided.

67. We have used the term 'need' on several occasions and feel that it requires some definition. The term is a confusing one; we use it to indicate the gap between the present state of an individual and the more desirable one to which he aspires. This concept can be applied to a community or to society as a whole. Needs in this sense are derived from an individual's way of life and his environment. He cannot always clearly recognise them nor can they be simply identified by external observation. Their identification emerges as a result of a process of interaction involving those thought to be in need and those able to provide for its satisfaction. Nor must it be assumed that the assessment of need is a once-and-for-all matter. It must be a continuing process and in regard to adult education is an essential one if provision is to be relevant.

SPECIFIC AIMS

68. In an attempt to define a clear role for adult education we have taken into account such factors as the growing technological basis of our society, the dehumanising aspect of many kinds of work and the impact of the mass media, all of which tend to erode individuality and paradoxically to increase a sense of isolation and alienation. There is therefore a growing need for opportunities which enable individuals to develop their capacities for a full and rich personal and social life and for educational provision to be directed at reducing to the minimum impediments to this development. Therefore we see *the reaffirmation of individuality* as the first aim of adult education.

69. Further the increasing range and sophistication of the products of modern technology, the sheer scale of its institutions and the complexities of modern bureaucratic processes make it more essential than ever to ensure that people have the necessary skill and knowledge to use to the full the resources of society. *The effective use of the resources of society* is a second aim.

70. In a society that encourages freedom of association and stresses the rights of the individual it is inevitable that groups of people will emerge whose common interests, problems or characteristics may be regarded, in some cases only initially, as those of a minority. Sometimes their attitudes will differ only in degree from that of the community at large; an organisation like Shelter, for example, highlights society's general if less active concern about housing conditions. Occasionally minority groups will have beliefs that differ more radically from those of contemporary society, as those of trades unions once did. In either case acceptance of the very existence of such dissenting groups entitles us to describe our society as pluralist and to

consider ourselves as living in a free community in which individuals have the right to unite with like-minded people and give expression to their opinions. This right to form groups, along with the right of opposition to and criticism of the government of the day and other forms of authority, is fundamental to a pluralist society. Such groups have a right to seek a share of the resources available for adult education whenever the purpose can reasonably be regarded as educational. *To foster the pluralist society* is a third aim.

71. The final aim we have identified is *education for change* itself. Many individuals wish to play a more active part in shaping their own physical and social environment. They seek opportunities to participate in the making of decisions that affect the facilities, amenities and organisations on which the quality of life very much depends. The institutions of society are undergoing continuous transformation and, while on some occasions these changes are willed by the individuals and groups most affected, on other occasions these individuals and groups are the reluctant victims. In both cases new ways of acting and new ways of learning must be developed.

We now make proposals for the kind of provision that will assist in the realisation of these several aims.

Reaffirmation of Individuality

Recreation
72. Each day many thousands of adults involve themselves in recreational activities. They may join a group or class for one of the many forms of physical recreation, a choral group or a music ensemble, a painting class or a class in ceramics, a class in conversational French or in dog obedience, a class in sewing, woodwork, literature, philosophy or one of a hundred others. Their motives in joining are many and varied—to acquire a new skill, to enjoy new activities, to keep abreast of social, political or cultural development, or simply to meet people. Over the country as a whole an impressive variety of activities appears to be provided. Local provision is limited however and is not always equally available to all. We are in no doubt that involvement in the kind of activities instanced here can add new dimensions to life. Providing bodies must ensure that provision is made at appropriate times and in appropriate places so that all members of the community from the most disadvantaged to the most gifted have access to these opportunities for self-fulfilment.

The Family
73. The family has always made important contributions to the education of the young and to social well-being generally and it is a matter of concern that its capacity to make these contributions may be reduced by the increasing stresses and strains placed upon it by social change and technological advance. Good parenthood requires an understanding of the physical, mental, emotional and social development of children and an awareness of the relative contributions of home and school to the child's education. Furthermore the creation of a home has financial and managerial as well as emotional aspects. Preparation for the responsibilities of parenthood starts in the school but opportunities for learning about these responsibilities and how to discharge them must continue to be provided until well into adult life. Already there is a demand for provision aimed at improving the quality of the family home, the quality of family life and the quality of the relations between and among members of the family. These demands will undoubtedly increase and provision must

therefore be made more widely available to all sections of the community. Activities and a programme directed at the family as a whole can contribute a great deal and should be further developed.

74. In almost all families there comes a time when the roles of parent and child are all but reversed. While the elderly parent is an individual in his own right and should be encouraged to participate in whatever educational facilities are provided we see no reason why the grown-up child should not be assisted to an understanding of the problems of the elderly.

The Elderly

75. Advances in medical and welfare services have had significant effects on the age structure of the population. An increasing proportion of the population is aged 60 or over. Many elderly people are active and are capable of using to the full whatever educational facilities are available to the community as a whole and should be encouraged to do so. Nevertheless the elderly retired person often has particular problems concerning, for example, health, change of status and the amount of leisure and so requires provision of a particular kind. Pre-retirement courses and retirement courses have developed over the last few years and we hope that this development will continue.

The Disadvantaged

76. Over the last decade or so attention to those at a disadvantage in our society has shown that their plight is due to a variety of social, economic, educational and personal deficiencies which, because they tend to be handed down from one generation to the next, are to a large extent self-perpetuating. Education alone cannot break this 'cycle of deprivation' but it has a role to play in altering the attitudes of adults caught up in it. Without an alteration in these attitudes the effects of any change in the physical environment might be nullified. This is an area of work where a co-ordinated approach involving housing, social work and health departments as well as education is clearly called for. It is also an area of work of high priority where costs will be relatively high and results slow to materialise.

The Handicapped

77. In our society there are some who differ from the majority in that they are affected by mental or physical handicap. The precise nature and extent of the handicap varies considerably as do the social and educational needs of the individuals concerned. Much is done to meet the educational needs of the handicapped who are still of school age but investigations carried out on our behalf show that little or nothing is being done to meet the special educational needs of the mentally or physically handicapped adult. Those who are able to do so are expected, rightly in our view, to take advantage of conventional adult education provision; those who cannot however are largely disregarded. Clearly this is an area of need which requires special attention.

Remedial Education

78. It is disappointing that in spite of the increasing length of schooling there is still a significant number of adults whose basic educational and social skills are inadequate. This inadequacy makes it difficult for them to secure and retain employment compatible with their true ability, reduces their

effectiveness as citizens and prevents them from exploiting to the full the opportunities of life. Facilities for remedial education, wider in content than those available in primary or secondary education, must be provided in post-school education in settings and with methods that take full account of the insecurity experienced by the adults concerned.

Effective Use of Resources

Consumer Education
79.   The major thrust of our economy is directed towards the production of consumer goods. Though many of these goods reach a high level of sophistication they are aimed at the ordinary man or woman. Competition to sell products results in high pressure salesmanship where the essential qualities of the product are hidden behind verbiage and hyperbole. The very size and impersonality of retail outlets make it difficult for consumers to be discriminating in their purchasing and difficult for them to register complaints. The rights of the consumer are being more widely recognised but protective legislation can be only partially effective in a situation where astute commercial brains are continuously looking for methods of increasing sales. Although there has been substantial provision of classes on decimalisation and Value Added Tax and specialised provision by voluntary organisations such as the Electrical Association for Women with their courses in the use of electricity, education for the consumer is an area which has been relatively neglected. Consumer education must concern itself with how to use, how to choose, how to distinguish fact from opinion, how to seek redress and how to bring pressure to bear on producers in the interests of the consumer.

80.   Large and growing numbers of people now buy articles on credit with very little idea of what the facility of credit is costing them. Many are quite unaware of how the rents of their houses are calculated, of the difference between rent and rates, of the comparative returns they get in satisfaction from the proportion of income which they spend on food, clothes, rent, rates, entertainment, holidays and so on. The complexities of the welfare state and the rights and obligations it brings are often little understood by those who should most benefit from it. Involvement in even the most minor way with officialdom can create acute feelings of uncertainty and anxiety among large sections of the population. We have recorded evidence that this is a vast area of unsatisfied educational need and we commend this to the attention of the providers of adult education.

Health Education
81.   The demands of society place on the individual a considerable stress both of a physical and of a mental nature and his ability to respond to them is greatly dependent on his state of health; yet it is only in pre-retirement or retirement courses that health education features prominently. There is need for educational provision directed at creating a more positive attitude to good health and a more sensitive understanding of physical and mental health. Provision of this kind should be extended to the various groups in the community with common health problems or hazards. Perhaps an even greater need is to ensure that all members of the community are fully informed about the interrelation of health, diet, work, exercise and the environment in which they live. Any programme of health education should concern itself

with the prevention of accidents and with the dangers of smoking, alcohol and drugs. Probably more than any other this area of education of adults requires co-ordination of effort, involving as it does different departments of local and central government as well as many voluntary organisations. Agencies of adult education generally must contribute more widely than in the past to the provision of opportunities leading to personal and community action to maximise the use of the available resources for the promotion of good health in all its physical, psychological and social manifestations.

Fostering the Pluralist Society

Industrial Relations

82.   The quality of industrial relations affects the lives and livelihoods of everyone. Human relations at work and collective bargaining form an area of activity which has not been backed by an educational provision adequate to prepare people for their involvement in it. This has been particularly true of the employee side of industrial relations with trades unions depending for most of their administrative skill and leadership at local level on the voluntary activity of branch officials and shop stewards. On the management side too there are still serious gaps in the educational provision for supervisors, foremen and those at higher levels of management who are directly involved in industrial relations, in many cases without an adequate understanding of the problems involved and the skills required to resolve them. This may be a deficiency in vocational rather than adult education and for that reason outwith our terms of reference. However this is an area in which we find it difficult clearly to draw such a distinction and we consider it appropriate for us to stress that there is a strong case for expanded provision of education for trade unionists, supervisors and management in the skills required in industrial relations. A Working Party on Shop Steward Education and Training in England and Wales, under the Chairmanship of Mr D J Gold, HM Inspector, reported in July 1972. Scottish Education Department Memorandum No 1/1974 drew attention to this Report and in particular to certain of its recommendations which were felt to be relevant to Scotland; and it encouraged action on them. Our own investigations (see Appendix XIV) indicate a growth in this provision since 1971 but although more colleges offer courses for shop stewards or plan to do so we believe that much more requires to be done. We make recommendations to this effect later in the report.

Immigrants and Foreign Workers

83.   The educational needs of immigrants and foreign workers are of two kinds: those relating to their parent culture and those concerned with their assimilation into the Scottish culture. There is little evidence in the public sector of any provision aimed specifically at maintaining the cultural life of the immigrant, yet if education is to meet the needs of all this is a very easily identifiable area of need. A number of bodies such as the Institut Francais d'Ecosse exist to further the interests of their own nationals and others attracted to their culture. Generally they demand a relatively high educational standard. The influx of greater numbers of foreign workers as a result of our membership of the European Economic Community or of the attractions of the oil industry will probably increase the demands for this kind of provision. Education for assimilation—and we prefer this term to integration—is provided readily for the children of immigrants. A knowledge of English is

clearly a pre-requisite to assimilation but little evidence was given to us to suggest that much in the way of provision of this kind is being made at present for adult immigrants. A few classes in 'English as a second language' were provided in some urban areas but these catered for only a few specific groups of non-English-speaking adults and did not elicit much response; one voluntary agency was developing a home-visiting scheme to teach English to immigrant Asian women. There is an obvious and urgent need for investigation into the particular educational needs of adult immigrants of all kinds and for appropriate provision to meet them.

Members of Voluntary Groups
84.   Our society has a great variety of organised voluntary groups, social, educational, sporting, religious or political in purpose, through which many adults find learning opportunities. Some of them may be entirely local in their operations and connections; others may as a result of affiliation or for other reasons have regional or national interests. Some receive assistance or advice from national bodies such as the Scottish Sports Council, the Scottish Arts Council, the Scottish Community Drama Association and the Association of Arts Centres in Scotland. The educational role performed by many of them, whether they are purely local or have national connections, is such as to bring them within what we have termed community education and consequently within the concern of the education authorities. These authorities already recognise the contribution voluntary groups make to a comprehensive education service and in a variety of ways help many of them to be effective. We have more to say about voluntary organisations in Chapter 10 but at this point we wish to record our view that it is desirable that the help given to them should be extended still more widely.

Education for Change

Community Development
85.   The process by which those who live in a community (defined in either geographical or social terms) are helped or encouraged to act together in tackling the problems which affect their lives has come to be called community development. Implicit in this process is the assumption that having been helped to solve one problem those involved will be sufficiently motivated and will have acquired sufficient skills to tackle other problems. The educational character of community development is therefore readily recognised and the youth and community service has long been involved in the process. Much less obvious is the precise role that the adult educationist should play in it. Involvement in community development calls into question traditional didactic approaches and emphasis on classes and class numbers; but it provides new opportunities for reaching large sections of the population hitherto untouched by adult education. Elsewhere in this report we refer to the need to place greater emphasis on the adult educationist's role of stimulating and promoting interest in adult education activities. The French aptly describe what we have in mind as 'animation'. Experiments along these lines undertaken by the Department of Educational Studies of the University of Edinburgh in the new town of Livingston have met with some success but have also highlighted the problems and difficulties involved. Adult education should participate increasingly in community development and much more experimentation is needed.

Social and Political Education

86. We received little evidence relating directly to social and political education. At one time subjects which were held to have a bearing on national and international affairs—civics, political science, current affairs, international relations—figured prominently in educational programmes. Although these subjects have declined in popularity there has been an expansion of provision related to specific civic functions—children's panels, lay magistrates, the professional social worker and the volunteer—or to more specific areas of public concern—'Caring for People', 'Drugs and the Community', 'Roots of Crime'. This kind of provision reflects a desire on the part of many people to involve and inform themselves about particular social issues. The WEA, trades unions and more recently some universities have undertaken programmes of trade union education. The Community Councils provided for in the Local Government (Scotland) Act 1973 ought to give many more people an opportunity to participate in their own local affairs. Provision in this area of adult education is still relatively meagre; there is some evidence that certain educational agencies are prepared to deal with controversial issues of public concern but in general not nearly enough is being done. Educational providers have here an opportunity and a responsibility to make real the concept of the participating democracy.

Development and the Environment

87. Urbanisation and industrial expansion impose hidden costs on the community. Greater demand for land can deny to sections of the community the amenity which they have enjoyed for years; exploitation of natural resources at local, national and global levels can affect present and future generations; pollution and the disposal of waste are problems that face both the ordinary householder and the industrial giant. Education has a responsibility to ensure that these hidden costs are made more widely known and more thoroughly understood. People who are directly concerned in any issue involving the environment need help to acquire the skills and the expertise required to present their case effectively. The complex industrial developments affecting Scotland at the present time will intensify the need for this kind of provision.

Bridging the Educational Gap

88. Major developments in educational policy, such as the raising of the school leaving age and advances in methods and practices in school education, can have the effect of widening the educational gap between the new generation which benefits directly from them and older people whose full-time schooling took place before they were introduced. At present those over the age of 40 who left school at the statutory leaving age have had a year's less schooling than those under 40, who left school after the age had been raised to 15. There will soon be a further group of adults who will have had full-time education up to 16. The education of the older generation was designed by and for a society which differed in many ways from that of today. It was less than adequate by present day standards and in some respects narrower than that received by younger people. In our view, therefore, major advance in school education should be accompanied by measures to help encourage older people to widen their education correspondingly. So far such measures as have been taken have been quite inadequate, and 'second chance' and continuing educational opportunities at all levels must be much more generally

available. At the level of higher education the Open University has demonstrated the truth of the adage that it is never too late to learn.

Professional Groups
89.   Opportunities to enable individuals to acquire new or additional professional or technical qualifications and for others to master new concepts and practices in their professions have been provided for many years in institutions of further and higher education. Of recent years many professional and quasi-professional bodies have been looking to adult education agencies also to make this kind of provision. A number of university extramural departments such as Glasgow are already providing refresher courses for professional groups. This growing awareness of the interest in continuing education for the professions will make increasing demands on adult education.

Understanding Science and Technology
90.   Our world is a complex one in which the relationships between science and technology and the various social and cultural activities of man must be widely understood and discussed. Without informed discussion and policies based upon such discussion more and more people will feel that they are recipients, even victims, of the consequences of change rather than members of a society which wills and controls the changes which are taking place. Adult education can make an important contribution towards avoiding such alienation. One of the most important of its roles should be the interpretation of science and its associated technologies to the non-scientist. Everyone is affected by scientific and technological developments yet few are able to make balanced judgements on the industrial and social implications of scientific discoveries and technological developments. In order to do so the non-scientist should learn something of the language of science and, even more importantly, appreciate the nature of scientific method and thought. Scientific developments will provide a main source of intellectual excitement in the coming decades. The opening up of this field to the wider public outside the universities, research establishments and other laboratories will become increasingly desirable and valued. This process of distilling and transmitting the essentials of scientific development deserves the attention of mature scientists of high calibre who are willing to forego the esoteric language of their specialisms and to relate science and technology to social philosophy and the arts. This is therefore an area in which the universities can make a particularly valuable contribution.

ATTRACTING AND MOTIVATING STUDENTS

91.   The kind of provision outlined above indicates what we mean by a comprehensive educational service for adults. Merely to provide classes or courses directed at meeting the kinds of needs identified however is not enough. Participation in adult education is still very much a minority interest but for providers to place the blame for this situation on the 'apathy' of the people they are seeking to serve 'is not only to congratulate oneself and criticise others—it is also to declare that there is no reason to look any further for explanations'. This quotation is from the Interim Report of the Department of Educational Studies, University of Edinburgh, on 'A Study of the Role of Adult Education and the University and its Potential Contribution to the

Community in Edinburgh and South-East Scotland' commissioned by the Committee. The report continues, 'Our research shows that further and more helpful explanations are readily available and that people's apathy towards what is at present offered in adult education must mean that they would accept activities which were educational if they were presented in a different way'.

92.   The perennial question for adult education is what compels adults to learn, for learning is work and sometimes hard work. The motives may be as numerous as the students attending—a sense of educational inadequacy, intellectual curiosity, vocational interest, a desire for companionship or simply to escape from the home. The apparent triviality of some of them should not be allowed to obscure the fact that they are very real to the individuals concerned. The extent to which these motives are satisfied during the early periods of attendance at classes will often determine the student's future attendance; but those which bring a person to the activity in the first place may not be strong enough to keep him there, much less cause him to continue to learn. There is now sufficient evidence to show that adults will be more highly motivated to learn if emphasis is placed on the applied rather than on the theoretical, if content is related to the performance of everyday tasks and obligations and if the methods used take into account their accumulated experience of life. Any statement of the aims of adult education such as we have just completed will be of little avail unless adults can be encouraged to pursue them.

COUNSELLING

93.   To capitalise on motivation, to maintain interest and to extend the horizons of the increasing number of adults we expect to respond to a revitalised service will demand a closer personal support of each adult student by the educationist. The counselling role already developing within the guidance system during the phase of initial education requires to be extended more effectively within adult education. Basically this will mean ensuring not only that opportunities for adult learning exist but that these opportunities are recognised and that people are assisted to choose the course or activity most relevant to their individual needs.

COMMUNITY EDUCATION

94.   At the beginning of this report, when defining terms, we said that 'Social, cultural, recreational and educational activities for adults are so interrelated that any attempt to distinguish between them or to deal with one without regard to the others would be undesirable even if it were possible'; and we adopted the term 'community education' to describe the wide spectrum of educational opportunities which these activities sponsored by a variety of statutory and voluntary agencies made available. It is our view that the aims we have proposed for adult education are practicable and achievable only if adult education is fostered and developed as an element of community education—an element which, while having characteristics and requirements specific to it, shares with the other elements common aims requiring for their accomplishment the collective resources and expertise of all the elements.

The spectrum is so wide that all the parts cannot be linked in one organisation and in some cases special arrangements will have to be made for co-operation and collaboration. This may for example be the most practicable way of dealing with the overlapping interests of education departments and the departments of leisure and recreation now emerging as a result of the Local Government (Scotland) Act 1973. However, we are convinced that it will be in the best interests of the adult education service, as well as of those it seeks to serve, if it is regarded and operates as part of a community education service which also embraces the youth and community service. Adult education and youth and community service already overlap and interrelate to a considerable extent; but there would be much advantage from still closer collaboration. Sections of the public hitherto virtually untouched by adult education would become more accessible and adult education would acquire valuable, committed allies in the large staff—full-time, part-time and voluntary —in the youth and community service. We have reason to believe too that the benefit would not be one-sided. The infusion of work of a more intellectual kind into the programmes of the youth and community service would we understand be welcomed by many of the workers in that service. Cross-fertilisation of ideas, methods and approaches would be of general benefit as would be the sharing and maximising of the use of resources and facilities. *We therefore recommend that adult education should be regarded as an aspect of community education and should, with the youth and community service, be incorporated into a community education service.*

SUMMARY OF AIMS

95. This Chapter has summarised our concept of adult education and the remainder of the report concerns itself with the implications. We have acted on our belief that education enables man to increase his understanding of his own nature, to develop to the full his potentialities and to participate in the shaping of his own future. Society need not fear that by stressing individuality we are sowing the seeds of anarchy for it is only where people have developed their own unique individualities that social ideals of the highest order emerge. Underlying our whole report is the mutual relationship between individual and social aims expressed so clearly by Sir Eric Ashby*: 'We live in a society which confers on the worker (irrespective of whether he is manual or clerical and irrespective of the amount of education he has) political responsibility, civic rights, and leisure. The contemporary problem in adult education is that among many people at all levels of education the leisure is without purpose, the civic rights are without significance, and the political responsibility is assumed without understanding. We are learning the hard way that social emancipation without personal emancipation is of little value. In a world noisy with the organs of mass communication and riddled with propaganda, modern man is hard put to it to preserve his status as an individual. To help preserve this status is the contemporary task for adult education'.** The 20 years that have passed since this was said have seen an intensification of these characteristics and the needs that arise from them.

*Now Lord Ashby.

**'The Pathology of Adult Education'—The William F Harvey Memorial lecture delivered at Birmingham on 24 March 1955.

7 Expansion and Development

THE CASE FOR EXPANSION

96. Our appraisal of the nature of change in the community resulting from powerful social and economic forces has provided the background for much of our investigation and discussion. It has exposed certain limitations in an educational process which in the past has been very closely geared to a system based on separate and self-contained stages. Against this pattern of change in the community the specific aims appropriate to the education of adults have been set out. The composition of the educational community of the future as we now see it will reflect much more completely the diversity identified in the social community. There will be a growing emphasis on continuing opportunity in an articulated system within which consideration of the educational needs of adults will have prominence and attention. The anticipation of adult needs and the detection of trends will, given the voluntary nature of much of adult education, ease the position of the adult who wants to find his place in the educational process once again at a time of his choosing. Attention of this kind too will help in the creation of an educated and informed adult population able to make its necessary contribution within a democratic system. Much that is already provided through the adult service is in response to particular educational and social needs and, improved by better presentation and facilities, this will undoubtedly continue. To suggest that this goes without saying is not to undervalue in any way the genuine achievements of the past and present. Any consideration of the adult education service required to meet the evolutionary situation which has been described must however look beyond a continuation of well-established practice.

MEASURES TO SECURE EXPANSION

97. The feature of the present position which calls most clearly for expansion is that very small fraction of the adult population which participates in adult education and the limited social range which that fraction covers. This is easy to say and easy to defend. To produce remedies which have any clear prospect of success is much more difficult. We have considered whether expansion could be secured by the prescription of standards of provision in Regulations issued by the Scottish Education Department or by the restoration of the pre-1956 position when education authorities were required by the Secretary of State in accordance with powers conferred on him by the Education (Scotland) Act 1946 to prepare and submit for his approval schemes for the provision of all forms of primary, secondary and further education. Voluntary leisure-time non-vocational further education was exempted from this requirement in 1956. Neither of these measures would in our view be appropriate. For a service like adult education which is being developed, which is dependent on individual interest and choice and which is properly subject to variation from area to area, standards of provision prescribed in Regulations would be too inflexible and too difficult to define or modify. Statutory schemes for the provision of adult education would present similar difficulties. Experience during the years immediately prior to 1956 showed that such schemes were of little value because local circumstances and ideas on informal further education changed more rapidly than schemes

could be amended and because financial restrictions prevented authorities from carrying out their schemes even when these had been formally approved. We consider that flexible, non-statutory development plans would be helpful and *we recommend that the Secretary of State should from time to time invite education authorities to inform him of their plans for the development of adult education along the lines agreed.* We would expect that the advice of the national council we propose later in this report would be sought on these development plans and that there would be subsequent discussion and consultation with the authorities and with other agencies involved.

98. Expansion of adult education may also be stimulated by financial measures and inducements. As regards expenditure by education authorities in respect of such expansion it appears to be most unlikely that a proposal for the introduction of specific grants from central Government for the purpose would be received favourably either by the Government or by the education authorities. The trend for some time has been to move away from specific grants towards a general grant. However, the present rate support grant system, by means of which Government grant is made available in block form to support the majority of local services provided by authorities, enables additional resources to be given to a particular service by general agreement between the Scottish Office and the local authority associations at the bi-annual negotiations about the total amount of rate support grant for the following two years. Because of the nature of the system there is no guarantee that every authority will use the additional resources for the particular service concerned; but there is evidence, for example in relation to the recent development of the youth and community service, that if it is accompanied by positive guidance from national level the making of provision in this way within the rate support grant system can be effective. *We recommend that such action be taken in respect of expenditure on the expansion of adult education.* Later in this report we also recommend the introduction of a new scheme of grants to voluntary organisations with the aim of assisting special developmental work (paragraph 212).

99. We hope that the numbers participating in adult education will increase as a result of the various suggestions and recommendations made in this report for the improvement and development of the service, but quite specific efforts to attract more people to adult education are called for. It is of the greatest importance that a deliberately planned and sustained attack be made on the problem by the education authorities with the full support of the Scottish Education Department on the one hand and the extra-mural departments and appropriate voluntary organisations on the other. An especially clear need exists for more and better market research to find out what particular subjects, themes, activities and methods of approach will prove attractive in different geographical areas and in different social milieux and there should be more investigation into the relationship in adult education between supply and demand. It is too readily assumed that demand must precede supply; experience shows that supply may well stimulate demand and acts of faith must increasingly be a feature of pioneering adult education.

SCALE OF EXPANSION

100. Given the voluntary character of participation in adult education, forecasts of future provision must necessarily be tentative and planning must be

flexible. We wish however to give an estimate of the magnitude of the expansion we consider desirable. In making our estimate we have taken a number of factors into account, starting with the present level of provision, comparing this with the level of student involvement we know to be achievable when greater resources are available to the providers and also taking into account the several aspects of provision to which we think special attention should be given. *On this basis we recommend the adoption of the aim of doubling the number of students by the mid-1980s.* The achievement of such an aim would mean that at most some eight per cent of the adult population would be involved in some form of adult education. Such an aim should be regarded as modest and certainly not over-ambitious. We believe that given time and adequate resources a much higher level of involvement should be possible. It is our firm view however that the expansion and increased involvement we recommend should mainly take the form of new development rather than simply an expansion of existing provision.

SPECIFIC AREAS FOR EXPANSION

101.   Besides the general expansion in numbers and social range which the foregoing paragraphs call for, there is a clamant need for development and expansion in many particular fields. We now comment upon some of the specific groups of people and aspects of provision to which we recommend special attention should be given.

Young Mothers

102.   The new personal situation in which young mothers find themselves presents particular educational needs and opportunities. Many of them may wish or require to revive skills and interests or to develop new ones. Often their needs are heightened by the attenuation of family ties and friendships which can result from living in new housing areas. Fortunately the expansion of pre-school education has been accompanied by an increasing interest among young parents in the process by which their children learn. This interest presents immediate opportunities for education and can be the starting point for the development of wider interests. Frequently their domestic situation is such that they are unable to take advantage of conventional provision.

103.   In addition many live in circumstances of marked social deprivation and need assistance, instruction and general support in coping with such problems of family life as low income budgeting and household care. They may also need, as others may, education for parenthood. Current provision to meet needs of these kinds is however extremely limited and must be improved. The area is one of obvious difficulty and if the education offered is to be acceptable and effective it must be marked by sensitivity of approach and informality of presentation. Facilities such as day-time centres and creches will be required and may be provided by various bodies. The co-operation of a variety of agencies will also be essential to make initial contact and to detect and assess needs. Indeed adult education will frequently play a support role for welfare and other services but its part in bridging the gap between education and the social services generally can be one of vital importance. *We recommend that there should be greater recognition than at present of the varied educational needs of young mothers and of the importance of ensuring that appro-*

priate provision is made to meet them. This is an area which offers opportunities for imaginative and rewarding development.

The Elderly

104. At the other end of the age scale are the elderly. Many people are now required to retire from their normal occupations at an age when they are still active, both physically and mentally, and likely to remain so for a number of years ahead. For some such people retirement can be little short of a tragedy, creating for them a mental and social vacuum and having a depressing effect on their morale. Domestically it presents them with an entirely new situation at a time in their lives when they are] least adaptable to change. Changing social patterns may mean that the ties with their own family are less closely knit and, though some have acquired the resources to adjust, others have not. The particular initiative on preparation for retirement and living in retirement which has come from the Glasgow Retirement Council is highly commendable, as is the co-operation which that organisation has received from certain education authorities and voluntary organisations such as the WEA. There is evidence that the courses, classes and conferences which have been provided have offered fresh interest and given a sense of purpose which have been to the benefit of the individual and to the general well-being of society. *But provision of this kind is not as widespread as it should be and we recommend that steps be taken to extend it to all parts of the country.*

105. *We also recommend that the elderly should be encouraged and assisted to become involved in adult education and community activities in circumstances which provide them with ample opportunity for social contact.* There will be many however who because of infirmity or immobility or various other reasons will require some special kind of provision to be made for them. Day-time activities will be necessary for those who may be reluctant to leave their homes in the evenings, particularly during the winter; and for those less mobile provision in close proximity to their homes will often be the only answer. Indeed, small scale, localised provision may be best for all kinds of elderly people. In the course of our visits to areas furth of Scotland we observed educational provision for the elderly in a residential home for old people and even within large blocks of flats and were very impressed by the response and the results.

Adults Working Unsocial Hours

106. An increasing number of adults now find that the nature of their employment requires them to work what are now described as unsocial hours, ie at hours which effectively prevent them from participating in many social and recreational activities which most others take for granted. They include many who are employed in essential public services such as the police, fire, hospital, ambulance and transport services or in the catering or entertainment industries. They also include shift workers in the coal, power and manufacturing and other industries whose hours of duty may vary from week to week. Yet, we have received no evidence to suggest that any serious efforts have been made to provide for the educational needs of these very large groups who are not in a position to take advantage of normal adult education provision. Day-time provision would probably be convenient for the great majority of them but special arrangements would be necessary for shift workers. This seems to us to be a very large area of opportunity urgently in need of investigation and development. *We recommend that education*

authorities should be required to ensure that adequate alternative educational provision is made, at convenient times, for adults who are prevented from taking advantage of normal provision because of the hours of their employment.

Adult Immigrants
107. We have already mentioned the need for investigation into the educational needs of adult immigrants as an essential part of the process of their assimilation into our culture. The available evidence suggests that little is being done at present to provide for this complicated area of need. *We recommend that education authorities, in consultation with the Community Relations Council and any involved voluntary organisations, should initiate such investigation and take urgent steps to secure the educational provision which the investigation shows to be necessary.*

The Disadvantaged
108. We have dealt above with some of the more obvious areas where expansion is called for and where much might be done within the established fabric of adult services. There are however other sections of the adult community at present inadequately provided for, groups who for a wide variety of reasons are unable, even if they so wish, to take advantage of conventional forms of provision. They include those who are at a disadvantage because of educational limitations or through mental or physical handicap, and those who find themselves in social, cultural or linguistic situations where they are in a position of disadvantage. A comprehensive and exhaustive account of these groups cannot be attempted but evidence submitted to the Committee and the experience of our visiting parties show that particular adult groups undoubtedly stand in special need.

Illiterate Adults
109. One such group consists of adults who are illiterate or who have a very limited literacy. Press publicity in the Committee's early days brought letters from parents, relatives and friends begging for help for adults severely handicapped both in regard to employment and in normal day-to-day living by limited capacities to read, write and count. Even more compelling were the letters and visits from limited literates themselves. Despite great difficulty they managed to convey the personal distress and misery they experience daily through their inability to cope with situations involving basic skills which most of us take for granted. We have reason to believe, though there is no firm evidence, that the number of adults of limited literacy in Scotland is much greater than is generally realised. It is the duty of society as a matter of social justice to ensure that those who are in this situation and wish to pull out of it should be given the opportunity to do so. The adult illiterate is just as much entitled to help as the well qualified school leaver seeking higher education. To meet his need will call for great care, considerable expertise and increased resources. Experience elsewhere has demonstrated that the motivation of the adult illiterate will carry him a long way in a relatively short time, given the opportunity to learn in a sympathetic atmosphere and in circumstances which do not publicise his deficiencies. *We recommend that education authorities should take urgent steps to make adequate and appropriate provision to assist adults with literacy problems and to make it known to those concerned by every means possible that such provision is available.* In this particular

connection we suggest that the use of the broadcasting media might be of special value.

Inmates of Penal Establishments
110. The Committee were brought face to face with a further aspect of the problem of illiteracy in adults through visits paid to penal institutions during 1972. These covered a closed prison, a Borstal and a Young Offenders' Institution. In each of them contact with prison staff and with inmates quickly confirmed a relationship between low literacy levels and the sense of inadequacy which lies behind much social deviation and propensity towards crime. This is not to suggest of course that there are no other contributory factors which lie outside the limits of our remit. In each of the establishments visited some adult education provision was made, mainly in the form of general education and remedial classes. Attendance was optional and spasmodic. There was some correspondence course provision. In only one case however was a trained teacher available on a full-time basis. The bulk of the teaching was carried out by prison staff, none of whom had had any kind of teacher training. Some assistance was given by lecturers and instructors provided by education authorities and other bodies. In general however the provision lacked professionalism, the accommodation was makeshift and unattractive and the resources limited.

111. We noted the expressed views of the prison staff that whatever they were able to achieve by way of encouraging prisoners to an understanding of the value of educational improvement would be likely to disappear again very quickly on a prisoner's release because of a lack of suitable follow-up arrangements. *We recommend that it should be an important part of any after-care service that prisoners who have made educational progress while in detention, whether in the skills of literacy or in some particular subject or skill, should on release be put in contact with educational agencies which can help keep alive and develop their interest and motivation.* There is no pious expectation that this alone will solve the problem of crime in contemporary society; but we believe that assistance towards a level of educational attainment not previously achieved may give some offenders the confidence and the necessary social skills to make genuine efforts at a fresh start.

112. From enquiries made we gathered that the situation in the establishments visited broadly reflected the educational position in penal establishments throughout Scotland and our concern was so great that we made immediate representations to the Prisons Division of the Scottish Home and Health Department. We were informed that the position was recognised as not being satisfactory and that the absence of adequate and continuing professional assistance prevented a proper assessment of the educational needs and potential of inmates; and we received assurances that efforts were being made to improve the situation.

113. The present position is that there are only five trained teachers employed full-time in the penal service: two of them in Borstal institutions, two in prisons and one in a detention centre. Otherwise such adult education as is provided is carried out by prison officers and by part-time lecturers and instructors provided through education authorities and others. The amount and range of provision varies a good deal from one establishment to another

and depends to too large an extent on the personal initiative and enthusiasm of individual members of staff. In November 1973 however a conference of Prison Governors on education, agreed on the need for the appointment in most if not all penal establishments in Scotland of a qualified teacher to serve on either a full-time or a part-time basis as Education Officer (an arrangement which already exists in other parts of the United Kingdom) and for the appointment of a Chief Education Officer at Prison Headquarters with responsibility for the development and direction of an effective education service, including adult education, within the penal system in Scotland.

114. *We strongly support the objects of these proposals and would urge all concerned to pursue them without delay. We would point out however that the need in most penal establishments is for a person qualified by experience and if possible by training to undertake the education of adults.*

The Handicapped
115. We paid particular attention to the position of those adults who through some form of mental or physical incapacity have difficulty in taking advantage of normal arrangements for education or are not able to do so at all. Three distinct categories were recognised: the mentally handicapped; the mentally ill; the chronic sick and disabled; and, within each of these, distinction must be made between those who are confined to hospital or similar institutional care and those who are in other forms of community care. Each group presents its own particular needs and there is the added complication that none stands as a distinct homogeneous group, so that the needs of each are varied and complex. Extensive inquiries were made of staff both medical and non-medical and of officials of many hospitals, and of the various statutory and voluntary agencies concerned with the health, education and welfare of those in residential care and in community care. These inquiries highlighted certain special features.

116. In none of these categories is enough use being made of education to better the condition of the handicapped. Unfortunately any kind of quantification of provision or need was virtually impossible because of the scale of the task and the difficulty of making distinctions, for example in the case of the mentally ill and the long-stay physically handicapped, between education undertaken voluntarily for recreative purposes and education for remedial or therapeutic purposes. Some indication of the scale of the problem is given by the estimate we have received that in some 160 hospitals in Scotland, varying in size from 20 to 1,800 bed capacity, there are at present approximately 36,000 long-stay beds occupied by geriatric patients, chronic sick (16–65 years of age, with two-thirds in the 45–60 age range) and those with multiple disabilities, including mental disorder. This however leaves out of account what we believe to be the vastly greater number of handicapped adults who are not in institutional care. The need is undoubtedly great in terms of numbers and there was agreement in the evidence to us that in very many cases considerable value could accrue to the handicapped person from the stimulation, social training and purposeful occupation which would come from participation in a programme of education.

117. Because of the complicated nature of the problems surrounding the handicapped there is a need for a clearing house or a focal agency where necessary action can be initiated and co-ordinated. At the present time too

much is left to individuals who are already heavily committed and whose enthusiasm cannot be fully effective because of their lack of knowledge of available resources. In this connection Scottish Hospital Memorandum 22/1972 which dealt with the Appointment of Organisers of Voluntary Services in Hospitals appears to us to offer a promising development. It is hoped that administrative reorganisation of the Health Service and of local government will lead to improved co-ordination of all agencies concerned with health, welfare and education of sick and disabled persons in both residential and community care.

118. The mentally handicapped whether in institutional or community care present very special problems. At a basic level there is a need for reading material on adult subjects in a form geared to their interests, intelligence and degree of literacy. Changing social features such as the introduction of decimalisation and metrication present particular problems for this kind of adult. The experience of the special schools and occupational centres indicates that many mentally handicapped children can profit by the educational and social experience which comes for example through learning to swim or through learning country dancing or from taking part in simple competitive games. There is a clear need to adopt a similar approach to the education of the handicapped adult.

119. Hospital authorities speak highly of the therapeutic and general benefit which comes from such educational provision as they have been able to develop with the assistance of education authorities, extra-mural departments, voluntary organisations and individuals. But it is generally made on a fairly piecemeal basis and a more co-ordinated approach is highly desirable. We consider that proper provision would stimulate demand, especially in the fields of arts and crafts and in the basic skills of reading and writing. The service is clearly capable of considerable improvement and expansion. Fortunately the established contacts with the organising staff in education, who can supply tho professional expertise and direction necessary for such improvement, provide a foundation for future development. As far as those in general community care are concerned the scale of the problem is such that only close co-operation and co-ordination of effort between the educational services, the social work departments (which are now responsible for the community care of the mentally disordered) and the relevant voluntary organisations will bring about the necessary development.

120. Much of what we have said about the mentally ill and mentally handicapped applies also to the chronic sick and disabled in hospital care. For information on the physically handicapped in community care we were greatly assisted by a research study carried out on our behalf by Dr J B Barclay of the Department of Educational Studies at the University of Edinburgh. Its findings have already been published under the title 'Educational Facilities available for the Adult Disabled in Scotland' but it is desirable here to summarise the salient points. The study showed that except in a few areas classes are not organised by education authorities specifically for the disabled and in those instances where specific provision has been made it has generally been designed to meet the needs of a particular category of handicapped persons. In most areas the handicapped have either to join those classes which are offered under normal arrangements or do without. Many of those who are mobile do attend such classes but for many others the nature and extent of

their handicap makes this impracticable. The design of schools and other premises used for adult education purposes generally prevents the chair-bound person from attending. He is unable to cope with stairs without a good deal of help, which may not always be available, and the special toilet facilities which he requires are seldom provided. The problem of transport between home and centre is generally a critical one and very often one which under present circumstances cannot be overcome. In particular the study concluded : 'The replies have shown how little is known about the adult disabled in regard to his requirements or desires in the educational field. They also show how little the citizen in general and the architect, teacher, social worker and others in particular know about the disabled.'

121.   The contribution of the voluntary organisations particularly concerned with the physically handicapped can be a considerable one. However, even where specialist organisations are relatively well endowed and organised the magnitude of the task of helping the handicapped to fit into a system primarily designed for those more fortunate can mean much frustration and disappointment for many who have the will but lack the physical resources. Support and sympathetic co-operation from local authorities and other sources will be required on a much more extensive scale than hitherto.

122.   All three categories of handicapped adult create their particular problems in relation to the training of staff. Attention is drawn to the need to give teaching staff and instructors who work with handicapped adults, especially those concerned with the mentally ill and the mentally handicapped, some training to equip them to deal with the particular problems they may encounter. Workers and helpers associated with voluntary organisations have a need for training in the general administrative arrangements of the various services which can be called upon to give support in meeting the needs of special groups of adults.

123.   *We recommend that education authorities should be required to compile and maintain in association with social work departments a register of handicapped adult persons living within their areas*, whether at home or in hospital or in institutions of any other kind and whose incapacity is unlikely to be of short duration ; *and that they should co-operate with social work departments, organisers of voluntary services in hospitals, representative organisations for disabled groups and any other appropriate statutory or non-statutory organisations, in establishing the particular educational needs of such persons and to ensure that steps are taken to meet these needs*. This would of course require the kind of co-operation between the various community services which we regard as essential to the future well-being of our society.

Areas of Multiple Deprivation
124.   Many of the social problems which confront society and to some of which we have drawn attention are presented in an acute and concentrated form in particular localities within urban areas where disadvantage is widespread and multi-faceted and where the inhabitants tend to be caught up in a cycle of deprivation. Such areas call for intensive corporate effort by public services and voluntary agencies to break the cycle and to involve the residents in the regeneration of the area. Together with the other sectors of community education—and of the education service as a whole—adult education has an

important contribution to make to the performance of this vital task and *we recommend that in the deployment of resources high priority be given to it.*

Rural Areas

125.   The disadvantages under which adult education has to operate in rural areas are simple enough to identify. In the towns and cities population is concentrated; there is generally a good deal of accommodation available in schools, in adult and community centres and elsewhere; there is usually a sufficient supply of suitable people able to provide teaching or instruction in a fairly wide range of courses and activities. In the country areas the position is generally very different. Population is comparatively small or scattered and frequently both; and public transport facilities are either unsuitable as regards time or, much more likely nowadays, simply non-existent. The only accommodation available may be the local primary school or perhaps the village hall, neither necessarily entirely suitable, and the immediate area is unlikely to be self-sufficient in terms of teaching staff. In such circumstances it is seldom that even a moderately wide range of courses can be offered in a rural area and even those courses which are offered may attract limited numbers of enrolments. Weather conditions in winter add to the other difficulties mentioned in bringing about fluctuations in attendance. Bearing in mind that certain education authorities at present lay down a minimum number of enrolments for the starting of a class and a minimum number of student attendances for its continuance, many advertised rural classes either fail to start or at best run constant risk of termination. This in turn can act as a disincentive to joining such a class. Students who consider there to be a risk that a class will not last may decide against making the initial effort to join. *We recommend that such minima as are established in relation to class sizes should have full regard to the population density and distribution and other conditions in the area.*

126.   In our view it is essential to secure to the maximum extent possible that those living in rural areas should have the same adult educational opportunities as their urban counterparts. It has been rightly said that all children of school age whatever their circumstances should have equal educational opportunities and we think the time has come for this to be seen to be equally true for those over school age. It is a fact however that one of the consequences of providing equality of opportunity for those at school is to make the position of the post-school rural population more difficult. The constant process of centralisation of education has tended to attract away from many small communities the teachers from whom in the past much of the real leadership for developments in adult education has come. We have no wish to suggest that the process of centralisation of education is wrong in principle. On the contrary it has the advantage that it leads to the provision of greatly improved accommodation and equipment which we hope will more and more become available for adult use. We think it necessary however that there should be greater recognition than at present of the effects of this major change on the other educational needs of the rural areas.

127.   Steps should be taken to emphasise the importance for community purposes generally, including adult education purposes, of those rural schools which have a reasonably assured future. *We recommend that where there is a definite need and where it is practicable accommodation specially designed for adult and general community use should be provided as extensions*

to such primary schools. We also recommend that local part-time leadership from whatever source should be identified by education authorities and should be given the responsibility for discovering the most suitable personnel and accommodation available locally and for assisting in securing appropriate provision and the stimulation of new interests. This will require the education authority to give the support of its full-time organising staff to the task of co-ordinating local enterprise in the voluntary field with the authority's own provision. *We further recommend that these local leaders should be provided with in-service training courses to equip them with the necessary skills to carry out the tasks allotted to them and should be given appropriate payment.*

128.   So far as classes, courses and other educational activities are concerned we think that while classes held in the evenings will continue to suit the majority of students, consideration should be given to the possibility that it might be more convenient for some students to attend on a whole day basis. Where appropriate, whole day courses might possibly be held at weekends as is the practice with rural-based associations like the Scottish Women's Rural Institutes. Whatever provision is made in rural areas however the level of support it can command will depend to a large extent on whether transport is available or not. Despite increasing public mobility there are still many people without personal means of transport, including a large number of those who are at present non-participants in adult education. A solution to the transport problem is vital to the success of provision in rural areas. In accordance with our expressed views on the need to give equal educational opportunity to those living in rural areas *we recommend that arrangements should be made in appropriate circumstances for transport to be provided without cost to the student between his home and his local adult education centre.*

129.   *We recommend that those authorities with special problems of remote and isolated communities should examine the possibility of providing correspondence courses on a variety of subjects.* We are aware that such a system has been developed successfully in Finland, a country with a total population of rather less than that of Scotland and with considerably greater problems of distance and isolation. Given the will a no less successful system could be devised to meet particular Scottish needs and we have more to say about the possible advantages of the 'educational package' at a later stage.

Scottish Traditions and Culture
130.   There is abundant evidence of a growing interest on the part of the general public in the need for action to preserve and maintain what is best in Scottish traditions and culture. This is to be found in the steadily increasing number of cultural and amenity organisations, some with limited, short-term aims and others with wider and continuing interests, but all of them concerned with the kind of country that Scots, either true-born or by adoption, want to live in and to pass on to their descendants. Adult education already contributes to this movement by providing classes and courses in, for example, Scottish country dancing, local crafts and local history. But we regard the preservation and development of Scottish traditions and culture as so important to the future of Scotland that *we recommend that there should be a considerable expansion of provision in a wide range of traditional and cultural subjects* including for example domestic architecture, archaeology, art, including Celtic art, and Scottish literature, *and that special steps should be taken to encourage*

maximum student support. We see it as a duty of adult education not only to help make the public aware of what in their society and way of life is at risk but also to enable them to play a constructive and informed part in preserving and developing it. We also see this as a field particularly suited to co-operation between the education authorities and relevant voluntary organisations.

Gaelic

131.   In parts of rural Scotland, especially the island communities of the North West, Gaelic is in widespread daily use. It is primarily for the education authorities in these areas to attend directly to the needs of the Gaelic-speaking inhabitants. In this they get the support of appropriate voluntary organisation notably An Comunns Gaidhealach. In its evidence to us An Comunns indicated that while the greater part of its effort was directed towards Gaelic-speaking school children it was also interested in adult needs. Our attention was drawn to the fact that although classes in Gaelic are widely offered to adults, both native speakers and learners, these are almost entirely concerned with study of the Gaelic language. We understand that in recent years there have been only isolated instances of courses of study on any other subject being offered in the medium of Gaelic, even in the Gaelic-speaking areas. *It would seem to us important that if the language is to maintain its vitality greater encouragement must be given to its use as a medium for some at least of the various subjects offered in adult programmes in Gaelic-speaking areas, and we recommend accordingly.*

Participation in Civic Affairs

132.   Increasingly evident in recent years has been a demand by the public to be informed about and involved in current decisions of local government and other statutory bodies which affect their present lives. To some extent this has been encouraged by central Government as for example in the action taken on the Skeffington Report* and in the provision which has been made in the Local Government (Scotland) Act 1973 for community councils in the reorganised system of local government. However; citizen-participation in and influence on the decision of local government agencies can be effective only if the public understand the machinery of government and the legislative framework within which it operates. Without this knowledge increased participation leads to increased frustration and disillusionment. At the same time all those in local government, both elected representatives and officials, need to understand what citizen-participation involves. In this situation adult education has a major role to play and a variety of methods of contact and presentation will be necessary.

133.   A new institution known as the Planning Exchange has recently been established in Glasgow by the Centre for Environmental Studies and the Scottish Development Department. Its experimental programme includes study groups for councillors, professionals and voluntary organisations on the planning process, on the dissemination of information and on specific topical issues in local government planning. The programme also includes traditional-type courses on planning problems and policies, but a major emphasis is on helping both the planners and the planned to be better equipped to debate and decide on planning issues. The intention is to provide a neutral ground on which the various professional and interest groups can discuss problems

*'People and Planning' HMSO 75p.

and the differing professional approaches to them. Additionally attempts are being made to bring together small citizen groups, amenity societies, etc, for discussion of mutual problems. At present many of those bodies tend to work in isolation and know comparatively little of the experience of each other in tackling similar issues. At the same time a library and information service is being developed to serve community groups and all concerned with the planning process. It is too early to judge the success of this new institution but it is clearly an experiment in adult education which deserves support and which may show ways in which the adult education movement can respond to society's changing needs.

Problems of Anti-Social Behaviour

134.   We live in a period of increasing violence, a situation in which the community suffers innumerable acts of apparently inexplicable behaviour which have the effect of degrading the environment. We understand that at the time of writing vandalism alone is costing one Scottish education authority something of the order of £700,000 per year. The picture is one of destruction by fire, broken windows, shattered fences and proliferating graffiti, the total effect of which is to depress the quality of life. But the trouble is not confined to damage to property. In some instances it is also destructive of services. It is well-known that anti-social behaviour in some large housing schemes has made the lives of transport workers unbearable and created a situation in which the residents of affected areas are denied an essential service. Problems like this have no easy solution and call for the use of many skills. In a situation of this kind the educationist cannot stand aside. Standard means have not so far provided answers. The comparatively recent expansion of the youth and community service and the growing involvement of the schools in forms of community service have made some contribution but there is much scope for innovation and greater provision. In the organisation of community groups to examine the reasons for anti-social behaviour and to work out local solutions we see a clear task for the educationist. He should be involved in the provision of additional educational experiences of an informal nature and the introduction of experimental programmes for the young adult at local level.

135.   The Social Work (Scotland) Act 1968 (Section 12) places upon all local government social work departments a wide responsibility for community welfare. In discharging this responsibility the social worker is in a position to diagnose both individual and community needs, to focus community attention on this and other kinds of community problems and to enlist the aid of the educationist in dealing with it. In order to avoid the strong possibility of overlapping and the duplication of effort and resources and to bring together those with complementary skills *it is essential to forge the strongest possible links between the social worker and community educator and we recommend that steps be taken to bring this about.* Similar links are necessary with other community services such as housing, police and recreation. Close collaboration among all concerned will not only lead to the possibility of new approaches to contemporary social problems but will also create opportunities for adult education provision to be extended to individuals and to sections of the community inadequately served. Consideration will require to be given to problems arising from the fact that responsibility for related aspects of social and educational policy rests with different levels of local government. Co-operation needs to start with the authorities who alone can make it possible for their staffs fully to co-operate.

SUPPORTING SERVICES

136.   The resources for expansion of these kinds will have to include not only the education authorities, the extra-mural departments of the universities and the various avowedly educational voluntary associations, but also organisations and agencies not hitherto regarded as being directly concerned with adult education. These means of provision are examined in some detail later in this report (Chapter 10). At this stage however it is appropriate to give particular consideration to ways and means whereby any service to adults can achieve greater effect. We have in mind methods of contacting the adult public, evaluating what is provided and promoting research.

Market Research and Publicity

137.   According to evidence given to us very few education authorities or other agencies at present undertake any systematic market research among the adult public prior to preparing their annual programmes of activities. Such sounding of opinion as is carried out tends very much to be from existing participants so that the views of the non-involved and non-participating members of the adult community are not ascertained. It may be suggested that non-participation is in itself an indication of lack of interest in any form of educational activity but this is not the case. There are many adults in all walks of life who have acquired the capacity to maintain the process of self-education through reading and discussion, through selective viewing and listening, through travel and by many other means, without the need to participate in any form of organised educational programmes. In addition we have had evidence from various bodies and individuals and through our own visiting parties that non-participation often comes from an individual's lack of confidence in dealing with a public service or in his own ability to benefit or derive personal satisfaction from any form of educational experience. It is important that adults of this kind should be made aware of the range of opportunities open to them. It is even more important that the many adults who feel the need to take up self-education but lack the confidence to make necessary contacts be given all practicable direct encouragement and assistance to do so.

138.   Letters sent to the Committee following early press publicity showed that even among adults who had a desire to learn there were many who had only limited knowledge of how to set about it. Many were clearly unaware of how and where to make contact with local education offices or centres to obtain advice and information. In any society there will always be individuals who lack an awareness of features which are self-evident to others but it seems to us that in many instances this is simply a by-product of limited educational experience. There is a need to ensure that information about adult educational opportunities is brought to the attention of the entire community and particularly of those who could benefit most by taking advantage of the opportunities offered. The fleeting press announcement about adult education classes, the strictly matter-of-fact and sometimes confusing booklet, the unimaginative poster on public hoarding or bus window have minimal impact and influence only those who are on the alert to look for them. It is significant that the case studies carried out on our behalf in three education authority areas (see paragraph 36) revealed that the majority of adult students enrolled for the class of their choice as a result of word-of-mouth recommendation.

139.   At the same time we were encouraged by the enterprise and ingenuity shown by certain authorities (mostly furth in Scotland) in detecting new patterns of demand and devising new ways of publicising their programmes. A pull-out supplement in the local newspaper, the use of local radio, the setting up of an adult education information office in a city centre, the publicising of a telephone number to call for information or to make suggestions, the circulation of a specially prepared broadsheet are all examples of ways in which the adult education service can be given prominence and through which its value as a public service can be demonstrated.

140.   *We recommend that the detection of need and the development of an efficient information and advisory service should be a major task for the professional staff of an expanded education service for adults.* Effective publicity needs not only time and money but expert treatment. In this connection we think it might be of value to the service if it were to adopt an identifying symbol and we suggest that this might be considered. We also think it essential that there should be an efficient counselling service in all areas. It is not enough to publicise a wide range of classes and courses even if it is based on extensive market research. There will still be many who will require advice and assistance to enable them to select the particular course or courses best suited to their needs and who will require continuing support and guidance if they are to sustain their involvement in progressive study. *We recommend that an effective and efficient counselling service should also be regarded as a major and urgent task.*

Evaluation and Research
141.   Complementary to such a development designed to detect need and stimulate demand and to make and retain contact with a varied adult public is the need for a systematic approach to the evaluation of what is provided. It is our experience that too few providers at present undertake any kind of monitoring of what they have offered. The crude measurement which is provided through the disappearance of those adult students who 'vote with their feet' is accepted all too readily and seldom is there any inquiry into why they have done so. The conventional if inadequate measurement by examination common in other sectors of education has much less application, although there is evidence that to work to some form of goal or target is an important part of the motivation of some adults. It is nevertheless abundantly clear that much of the value of what is provided in adult education is lost because of a failure to communicate to students the general aims and particular educational objectives of courses and class activities. Similarly the setting of criteria for measuring progress or performance requires to be undertaken much more systematically than is the general practice. This whole question of the application of the systems approach in learning, by the selection and evaluation of methodology and teaching techniques and of methods of assessment, is related to the question of training on which we have much to say elsewhere. The expansion and development of adult education will identify where these lines of approach are particularly relevant.

142.   The nature of adult learning and the monitoring techniques appropriate to it are however only examples of topics which require much more exhaustive investigation. The amount of research into aspects of adult education in Scotland undertaken in recent years has been limited. The Scottish Council for Research in Education has told us that only rarely is a proposal particularly

related to adult requirements put forward for consideration. This may well reflect the relatively low status this sector of education has in the professional mind. *We therefore recommend an expansion of research into aspects of adult education* through the SCRE and other organisations with a particular commitment to research. We do so from the conviction that only the support of carefully conceived research programmes professionally carried out will enable the future pattern of provision to adjust effectively to the changing demands and pressures it will increasingly encounter.

TECHNIQUES

Broadcasting

143. Both the BBC's Charter and the Television Act of 1964 speak of broadcasting as a means of 'disseminating information, education and entertainment'. During their comparatively short existence the independent television companies have made variable but frequently significant contributions to adult education; and the BBC has a record of educational service that stretches back for well over forty years. In considering the role of broadcasting it is important to distinguish between output that is generally educative, ie material which has no conscious intention to educate but which will nevertheless affect the recipient's attitudes, sympathies and awareness, and output that is explicitly educational (in which case it is planned so that it leads stage by stage 'towards a progressive mastery or understanding of some skill or body of knowledge'.*) It is not always easy to distinguish between the 'educative' and the 'educational' in broadcasting and there is always a danger that in any argument of the case for the explicitly educational the value and importance of programmes which are incidentally educative may be overlooked.

A Fourth Television Channel

144. We have received evidence from individuals and organisations about the role and potential of television and radio in adult education. In particular, arguments have been put to us on the question whether there is a need for a fourth television channel and, if so, whether it should be devoted solely to educational programmes.

145. The educational arguments in favour of an additional channel include the following:

(a) there is clear evidence of a growing demand by adults for educational programmes of high quality and further evidence that this demand is likely to show steady increase in future;

(b) the ability of television to make a significant contribution towards meeting this demand is already established;

(c) television is a cost-effective method of meeting the needs of large numbers of students and potential students who find it difficult or impossible because of the nature of their employment, the isolation of their homes or physical or other handicap to attend classes organised on conventional lines;

(d) such educational programmes as are provided on the three existing channels are steadily being relegated to very late and other off-peak times which are suitable for only a limited proportion of those who wish to see

*Broadcasting: Further Memorandum on the Report of the Committee on Broadcasting Cmnd. 1893, December 1962.

them and which provide no opportunity for capturing the interest of those not already committed;

(e) the competing and growing needs of the various sectors of education exert further pressures which, unless more television time overall can be provided, must inevitably exacerbate present difficulties.

146. There are particular kinds of adult educational programmes which are especially appropriate to television eg programmes about the environment, conservation, design and the visual arts generally; and experience has shown that while language teaching may be less dependent on the visual medium it can be made substantially more effective and popular by television presentation. There is a need for expanded provision of programmes of these kinds. There is also a need for a greater frequency and regularity of programmes if the benefits of more intensive teaching are to be secured. Development along these lines is not possible however without an increase in the number of programme hours allocated to adult education and particularly in the number of hours at peak and near peak viewing times. *The only solution appears to us to be to provide an additional channel and thus secure an increase in the total number of viewing hours and we therefore recommend accordingly.*

147. There are opposing opinions on the further question whether the additional channel should be devoted exclusively to educational programmes, but having examined the arguments on both sides we are convinced that the advantages to be gained from a channel devoted to educational programmes would be outweighed by the disadvantages. We assume that such a channel if created would be expected to absorb all the educational programmes at present distributed among the existing channels and that the latter would thereafter concentrate on news, current affairs, general entertainment and indeed all the programmes which attract the bulk of the viewing public. If this were so the inevitable consequence would be a situation in which only those with a positive commitment to study would tune in to the educational channel. *We therefore recommend that any additional channel should not be devoted exclusively to educational programmes.* The existing diversity of provision should be maintained on all channels and any increase in distributing capacity provided by a fourth channel should be allocated with the growing needs of adult education in mind; and there should be clear and precise stipulations as to programme balance and the allocation of good viewing times. We are particularly concerned that adult educational programmes should be given more time in the evenings and at weekends when the average adult has leisure time available; that they should be transmitted at times which would enable classes and other activities to be based on them; and that they should be interspersed with general entertainment programmes in order that viewers might carry over from a news or entertainment programme to an educational programme and as a result develop an interest in the educational subject.

148. *We recommend that the additional channel should be based on the BBC rather than the independent companies, partly because of the former's recognised superiority in the field but also because this would provide greater scope for cross-linking with the other two BBC channels.* In addition however we feel that to have two commercial channels both striving to reach mass audiences in order to secure the advertising revenue necessary for their survival could lead to an undesirable lowering of programme standards; and

that the BBC might be forced into a corresponding lowering of standards simply to maintain its audience levels.

149. Against the possibility that a Government decision might have been taken on the question of a fourth channel before the completion of our report we decided to convey an outline of our views to the Secretary of State for Scotland. Copies of our letter and of his reply are contained in Appendix XVII.

Radio
150. Radio should not of course be overlooked. Already it makes a valuable contribution to education, including the education of adults. We firmly believe however that it could do more not only by providing more adult learning programmes overall but also by providing more programmes specially designed to meet the needs of those adults who for one reason or another are unable to take advantage of conventional adult education provision, ie housebound invalid or handicapped or elderly persons, and those who look after them and are housebound in consequence; the mothers of young families and the parents in one-parent families; the adult illiterates or limited literates who cannot be made aware by normal publicity methods of the opportunities available to them for tackling their problem. This is the age of the transistor, and radio perhaps even more than television offers a means of reaching out to many of those unable to be reached in any other way and informing them of the educational opportunities open to them and how they can most readily take advantage of them. We hope that the network of local radio stations now being developed throughout the country will see it as part of their duty towards those living in their areas, on whom their viability as commercial enterprises depends, to include in their transmissions at least a reasonable proportion of programmes with an adult educational content and a service of information about the adult educational facilities available locally.

Administration of Educational Broadcasting
151. We have also considered the implications for the administration of educational broadcasting generally of an increase in the amount of television time allocated to it. The various sectors of education, including pre-school, school, post-school, Open University and post-professional, make claims on broadcasting which are no doubt often conflicting and which will inevitably increase. *This suggests to us the desirability of setting up two new national bodies, one with executive functions, the other with 'watchdog' functions and both appointed by Government and we recommend accordingly.* The former, which might be called the Educational Broadcasting Authority, should have a small membership not predominantly educational in composition in order to avoid any suggestion of vested interests operating to the advantage of one sector of education at the expense of others. It should have responsibility for securing the most effective use of the broadcasting time available to it on both television and radio. It should have an annual budget provided by Government and have the power to buy programme time or be given an annual allocation of programme time on all channels, including time during peak hours. It should have power to determine educational programme policy, including the allocation of programme times among the various educational interests, and power to produce its own programmes or to sub-contract production on lines similar to those already adopted for the Open University. In addition it should be required to have particular regard to the varying needs of the different regions of the country. In suggesting this we have

in mind the need to safeguard the position of Scotland where now perhaps more than ever before there are great and growing difficulties of isolation on the one hand and rapid development on the other which are unique in the United Kingdom and which require special treatment of a kind to which the broadcasting media are capable of making an important contribution.

152.   As regards the watchdog body we are aware that there are already in existence various such bodies representing particular aspects or areas of education. We understand that these bodies operate largely independently of each other and we think it better that they should be replaced by a single body which should have within its membership representatives of the Scottish Education Department and the Department of Education and Science and of the various sectors of education. We would expect that the development councils recommended in the Report of the Committee on Adult Education in England and Wales* and those we recommend later in this report for Scotland would be represented on it. The task to be given to this body should be to maintain a general oversight over the work of the Educational Broadcasting Authority, to give assistance and advice on any matter relating to educational broadcasting at the request of the EBA and to submit an annual report to Government on the work of the EBA, including any suggestions or recommendations for the improvement of the service generally.

Programmes
153.   We now turn from the question of major administrative change in the pattern of educational broadcasting to what matters to the individual student: the programme he receives and the circumstances in which he receives it. For some the particular virtue of the broadcast educational programme is that it can be seen or listened to at home, that one need not be dependent upon access to a teaching centre or upon the existence locally of a group of like-minded students. Whilst undeniably there are large areas of adult education in which the social element is of considerable significance and participation in a group is part of the educational experience, equally there are many people to whom study is for preference an individual pursuit. For such people and in appropriate fields of study we would hope to see a considerable increase in the provision not only of broadcast teaching but of correspondence work related to series of radio or television programmes. Ten years ago the effectiveness of the conjunction of correspondence and broadcast teaching was demonstrated both in the experience of the National Extension College (complementing the educational provision of Anglia Television and at other times the BBC) and in the experimental course in Economics ('The Standard of Living') offered in 1964 by the University of Nottingham and ATV. The techniques which since that time have been vigorously expanded and refined by the Open University should be adapted to adult education in general; and it seems reasonable to expect that an Educational Broadcasting Authority such as we have proposed might encourage their application more widely.

154.   Before the war further education radio programmes were often directed primarily at 'listening groups'. More recently however adult education programme output on both radio and television has been aimed mostly at the individual in his home; but not infrequently a programme has a secondary use, either live or recorded, when adopted in a class situation as the core or specialist element round which group treatment and discussion is built.
*Adult Education: A Plan for Development (HMSO £1·90).

During recent years the availability of comparatively inexpensive videotape equipment has increased the technical possibilities of recording educational television programmes for subsequent study; and as a result of patient negotiation by the broadcasting authorities there are now fewer legal inhibitions on the re-use of such material in a strictly teaching context. It is to be hoped that some clarification of the law affecting copyright, coupled with the necessary contractual agreements between the broadcasters and the unions involved, will soon produce a situation in which a wider range of broadcast programmes (the educative rather than the educational) may also legally be recorded during transmission and reproduced for analysis and teaching purposes.

155.   A few years ago, with the development of cable networks for educational television in some of our larger centres of population—Glasgow and Inner London are outstanding examples—it seemed possible that such distribution systems might spread throughout the country and that they might have significance for work outside the primary and secondary levels. For economic and other reasons however this has not come about. Instead there has been the development of the videocassette which may well revolutionise the distribution of visual material. The videocassette makes it possible for an individual possessing virtually no technical expertise to record broadcast material from an ordinary television receiver and reproduce it at will on any other television receiver. It also opens the way to a much easier re-use of the growing amount of television teaching material now being produced in colleges and universities, much of it suitable for work in the adult education sector. Commercially produced cassettes may well add to the stock of reference material relevant to adult work. While considerations of cost must be taken into account it does seem likely that the videocassette recorder, judiciously used, will prove a most stimulating addition to the equipment and resources of any adult education centre.

Other Audio and Visual Aids

156.   The lantern lecture was for long an established feature of the educational and cultural scene. It has been largely replaced by the tape/slide presentation in which the lantern slides have become 'transparencies' and the lecture or talk is reproduced from a magnetic tape. After what was perhaps excessive attention to the expensive television medium in the mid-1960's there is now a revival of interest at all levels of education in the teaching role of slides and/or straight-forward sound recording. There are many areas of study in which a tape-slide programme, made available to the student for individual intensive work, is highly appropriate. A more elaborate and costly extension of the same idea leads to the provision of programmed learning facilities such as are offered at certain further education colleges in Fife and Edinburgh where students can book in by appointment and pursue self-instructional courses. We commend the adaptation and application of such systems to suitable areas of adult education. They make expert teaching available to the student at whatever time of day and season of the year best suited to him and at a pace controlled by his own preference and capacity.

157.   Currently in favour is the 'educational package' which may include printed text, simple experimental material, transparencies, audio-tape and film loops: a hybrid assortment of teaching material in which each element is peculiarly appropriate to one aspect or another of the ground to be covered.

The combination of printed text, work assignment and broadcast material which is a distinctive feature of the Open University's presentation is a particular example. It is easy to recognise the effectiveness of educational packages of this kind since initially at least they will both represent and stimulate a good deal of new thinking about the material and the best method for its presentation. The application of educational technology in this way to the future pattern of adult education may well be of major importance. This technology will be at its best when its constituent techniques have been summoned to meet current and genuinely experienced problems in teaching and learning.

8 Statutory Responsibility

158. Under present arrangements statutory responsibility for securing the provision of facilities for the non-vocational education of adults in their leisure time rests solely with the education authorities. The Education (Scotland) Acts impose upon them a duty to secure that there is made for their area adequate and efficient provision of school education and further education; and further education is defined as including 'voluntary part-time and full-time courses of instruction for persons over school age'. In discharging this duty, as we have earlier explained, the education authorities generally provide at their own hand a wide range of classes and courses and co-operate with university extra-mural departments, the WEA and other voluntary organisations in securing the provision of other courses related to or derived from the various established university disciplines. It has been put to us that the power to make direct provision and receive financial aid from public funds in respect of it should be extended to the university extra-mural departments, the WEA and other approved voluntary organisations in the same way as in England and Wales; and that the absence of such power inhibits these organisations and restricts the development of the service as a whole.

159. We have carefully examined these views. We are not convinced that effective development of the service can best be achieved by granting to agencies other than the education authorities the power to make direct provision on the same basis as operates in England and Wales. As we see it the important thing is to obtain the goodwill and determined support of all concerned with adult provision, at whatever level and in whatever capacity. Given these essential pre-requisites we see no reason why development of the service should not be secured just as effectively under the existing arrangements as under any other. It seems to us to be undesirable to diminish in any way the responsibility education authorities have or feel for adult education. They are the main providers of education, they alone of the agencies involved deploy the wealth and variety of resources necessary for large-scale development, and they are uniquely situated to secure the continuity of educational opportunity which the future demands.

160. *We therefore recommend that statutory responsibility for adult education provision should continue to be vested solely in the education authorities.*

In doing so we wish to make it clear that while we expect the education authorities to expand the provision they make themselves we also expect them to increase their co-operation with and support of other organisations actively engaged in adult education with a view to a more effective use of the resources and expertise of these organisations. We also have in mind an expansion of the arrangements under which these organisations can secure grant assistance from central sources. We have more to say about this later in our report.

9 A Scottish Council for Community Education

161.   We consider that the steady development of adult education requires continuous oversight by a national council which would advise the Secretary of State and the statutory and other organisations concerned in all matters relating to adult education, would encourage close co-operation among these bodies, and would promote the adult education service generally.

162.   The Scottish Institute of Adult Education already seeks to carry out some at least of these functions. It has acted as a forum for the discussion of adult education matters and has provided much valuable advice and guidance in its various publications including the Report of its Working Party on Adult Education in Scotland, published in 1968. It is however a voluntary association of bodies and individuals concerned with adult education and is responsible only to its members. It is not in our view constitutionally suitable for discharging the wider tasks we have in mind. These require a much smaller body whose members would be appointed by the Secretary of State and would be responsible only to him. Such a body would not replace the Institute which would continue as the organisation representing those operating the adult education service or having a professional or personal interest in it. The need for such an organisation will remain.

163.   Moreover if a properly integrated community education service is to develop we think that the national council should be concerned with all aspects of it, youth and community service as well as adult education. We understand that this view is shared by the Standing Consultative Council on Youth and Community Service which at present advises the Secretary of State on matters concerning that service and is charged with promoting its development. We have been impressed by the way in which the youth and community service has developed in recent years under the guidance of the Standing Consultative Council and we consider that the future of adult education could best be secured by establishment of a new body on similar lines but with responsibilities covering both adult education and youth and community service.

164.   *We therefore recommend that the Secretary of State should establish a Scottish Council for Community Education* to assume the present functions of the Standing Consultative Council and in addition to carry out for adult education the functions outlined in the following paragraph. The members

should be appointed by the Secretary of State and should be selected for the personal qualities they can be expected to bring to the work of the Council rather than as representatives of particular associations or groups; but the Council as a whole should be broadly representative of the various interests concerned with community education. It should also include some members with other relevant interests. The Council should have its own staff, including a chief officer who should maintain close contact with developments in community education. Its expenditure should be met by the Secretary of State.

165.   The functions of the Council which come within the purview of this report should include:

i.   advising the Secretary of State and the statutory and other bodies concerned on all matters relating to the voluntary leisure time education of adults;

ii.   promoting a comprehensive leisure time educational service for adults and reviewing standards of provision;

iii.   promoting and co-ordinating research or development projects in adult education and advising the Secretary of State on applications for such projects;

iv.   keeping under review arrangements for the recruitment and training of staff for the service, including teachers, tutors and administrators, both full-time and part-time;

v.   promoting conferences, seminars and study tours for those directly concerned with adult education so that they may be kept informed of new developments, needs and techniques relevant to their professional responsibilities;

vi.   advising on the design and planning of centres for the education of adults, including experimental units;

vii.   promoting a central reference library, resource centre and information service for adult education.

166.   As we have said the Council would also be concerned with the other aspects of community education, particularly the youth and community service, and its membership should reflect this broad area of interest. In exercising its functions we would expect it to co-operate with existing agencies in the community education field and to make use of their resources where appropriate. Since the Scottish Institute of Adult Education in particular has, in the absence of any other national body and within its limited resources, carried out valuable promotional work the Council for Community Education will no doubt wish to work closely with the Institute. In research we would expect it to make use of the resources of the Scottish Council for Research in Education as well as those of the Institute and the universities. In promoting a resource centre and information service, the Council should, we think, consider with the Institute and with the Board for Information on Youth and Community Service whether the resource and information services which these two bodies now provide could be combined in one service for community education as a whole.

10 Agencies, Channels and Resources

167. The educational needs of adults are very varied. They range from those of the illiterate to those of the most gifted ; from those of seekers after improved qualifications to those of people looking for more satisfying ways of using their leisure. If it is to be comprehensive, provision for them must include opportunities to acquire basic educational skills and to pursue the discipline of the traditional liberal arts ; opportunities to reach a better understanding of personal and family problems ; opportunities for hobbies and recreational activities as well as for activities directed at the welfare of the community. Already, to meet these diverse needs, a wide variety of institutions and organisations, of subjects and approaches have been developed and they will have to be maintained and in some respects extended. The future however calls for a degree of co-operation and collaboration not hitherto attained.

168. In this section of the report we discuss separately the various bodies involved. This is done for convenience at the cost of some duplication but we would emphasise that for maximum effectiveness each body must be dependent to some degree on others. This interdependence is recognised in our later proposals for facilitating the collaboration and co-operation we regard as essential.

EDUCATION AUTHORITIES

169. If adult education is to meet the growing demands placed on it, it is of critical importance that leadership and initiative be exercised by the education authority whatever the strength and enthusiasm of relevant voluntary and other bodies in the area. (Ironically, during our consideration of this very point our attention was drawn to Press reports of a decision by an education authority to suspend all adult education provision within its area as the most simple and expedient way of effecting a specified reduction in their education estimates for 1973/74).

170. We have shown elsewhere that education authorities directly provide more courses for a greater number of adults than all the other providers together. This in itself does not necessarily mean that they provide a great deal ; and the general statement hides considerable variations in the scale of provision. Even the most active education authority must ask itself whether all the adult population within its area, including those who are disadvantaged, have reasonable access to educational facilities at suitable times and convenient places.

Range of Provision
171. Most education authorities distinguish quite clearly between activities of a practical and recreational nature such as crafts, domestic arts, and physical activities and those of a more intellectual kind, reserving the former for provision at their own hand and leaving the latter to agencies such as university extra-mural departments. We have already accepted elsewhere that there are

administrative if not educational reasons for treating separately those seeking to equip themselves for occupations in commerce and industry through a nationally organised system of courses in institutions of further and higher education but we cannot see any justification for this further division. The artificial distinction between the intellectual and the practical and recreational, based only on tradition and adhered to more rigorously in Scotland than elsewhere, is too restrictive on education authorities. While they should always have regard to the availability of organisations able and willing to mount courses of any kind on their behalf, education authorities must themselves feel free to provide directly for the whole range of educational experiences—recreational, creative, physical and intellectual—to ensure that educational experiences of all kinds are available equally to all. The word 'equally' has been here used deliberately. Many adults are intimidated less by the nature of the subject offered than by the place in which the class is provided. To many adults, especially those with minimum formal schooling, classes held in a community centre could be more attractive than those held in a university.

Maximising the use of Resources

172.   Given the resources at their command and a willingness to use them, education authorities have tremendous opportunities to meet the varied needs of adults. On the one hand they have at their disposal a wide range of accommodation and equipment and on the other the considerable range and number of staff—technical, professional, and academic—employed in schools and institutions of further and higher education. Arrangements must be made which will ensure full use of these facilities and of the energies and skills of those able and willing to participate in the different but no less challenging sector of community education. Significant success in this direction has already been achieved in those institutions in which an individual has been given specific responsibility for promoting 'intra' and 'extra' mural education for adults. In some comprehensive secondary schools the appointment of youth and community workers has resulted in extensive and intensive use of the school facilities for the education of adults, mainly in the field of recreative activities. As we indicated earlier one education authority has attached full-time staff to colleges of further education and given them responsibility for adult education. We have received evidence that this has produced encouraging results in the number and range of classes both in the colleges concerned and in centres near to them. Many of the teachers involved are themselves members of the teaching staff of the institutions concerned. The use of staff in this way strengthens links and creates understanding between different sections of education and brings the institutions themselves into closer contact with the community.

Administrative Arrangements

173.   The achievement of a level of provision which we would consider adequate for the education of adults requires an energetic promotional approach by all bodies involved in the field of adult education but the major responsibility for it rests with education authorities. Our observations in England and elsewhere and our awareness of the development of adult education by those education authorities in Scotland who have employed full-time adult education staff as tutors and/or organisers leave no doubt in our minds that, if adult education in Scotland is to expand and develop to the extent we envisage, education authorities will require to employ considerably more full-time staff trained for and experienced in adult education.

174. We deal in a later Chapter with the general question of staff. Here we would emphasise that within the education authority initiative and drive must come from the top if the education of adults is to receive the attention and resources it requires. With this in mind *we recommend that there should be in each education authority an officer of at least assistant director of education grade whose sole duty is that of securing that facilities for community education are adequate and efficient within his area.* Such an officer must make himself fully aware of the complex network of agencies which contribute to the education of adults, and in advising on the formulation of policies should take full account of the contribution which each is capable of making. He must be supported by an adequate number of qualified staff with the aim of ensuring that the total resources available are co-ordinated in the interests of a comprehensive and efficient service. We would expect some of the staff to be employed full-time on adult education, for example as organisers or as principals of major centres; but there will be others who though full-time employees of the authority have only a partial or part-time commitment to adult education. This group includes the heads of evening centres, the wardens of community centres and other youth and community workers. Coming as they do into direct contact with the adult community they have a major role to play in stimulating interest and in ascertaining and providing for individual needs. Some such staff already undertake these tasks but additional effort must be made to ensure that they fully appreciate the nature and significance of the part they can play in the developing field of adult education and are enabled by appropriate training to play it.

175. Variation in educational policies and in the educational resources available to them make it unrealistic to expect all authorities to administer their adult service in the same way. Nonetheless it is highly desirable that each should examine its own arrangements to see how and to what extent its present administrative practice facilitates or hinders the provision of a comprehensive adult service and should make such adjustments as may be necessary to ensure maximum efficiency. The complementary and overlapping nature of much that is carried out as 'informal further education', 'adult education', 'youth and community work' or 'community education' has led us, as we indicated in paragraph 94 to the important conclusion that a unified and enlarged community education service should be created. The implications of this conclusion are reflected in later parts of this report.

THE UNIVERSITIES AND THE EXTRA-MURAL DEPARTMENTS

Widening the Impact
176. Within the view we take of the education of adults a university will serve only a minority of participants but it is through the university that the highest level of academic study can be made available. For those seeking a disciplined approach to the acquisition of knowledge, for those seeking to pursue a subject to the bounds of knowledge and for those seeking to develop their intellectual faculties to the full, the university will continue to be the main source of satisfaction. The opportunity to develop individual interest through courses in liberal education has long been the major contribution of the universities. Up to the present however the impact of university extra-

mural provision on large sections of the population, particularly in urban areas, has been slight, though many within these sections are capable of study at this level. This is a challenge which the universities have shown themselves willing to meet and in recent years attempts have been made to establish extra-mural classes in some city housing areas though with only limited success. We have suggested elsewhere that the difficulty may be one of approach and perhaps of method rather than of subject matter and intellectual attainment. We have also suggested elsewhere the value of a community development approach in stimulating the demand for adult education, and *we recommend that the universities should develop this kind of approach*. We recognise that this will require a substantial injection of resources of all kinds.

Promotion and Organisation
177.   The practice of employing members of staff to extend the specific contribution of the universities to a wider public is a feature of the provision of extra-mural education. Such staff may on the one hand organise lecture courses, seminars and conferences and on the other lecture on subjects from within their own discipline, the balance between these different activities depending upon local needs and opportunities. To enlarge the contribution of a university within a particular area will require that increasing emphasis should be placed upon promotion and organisation, which must be undertaken in close collaboration with the relevant education authority. The universities have a wealth of intellectual and teaching talent which will be more widely utilised only if specialist attention is given to such promotion and organisation and *we recommend that the education authorities and the regional advisory councils (see paragraph 209) should support additional appointments to make this possible*.

Courses for Professional Groups
178.   The provision of academically based liberal education on behalf of the education authority and other bodies is by no means the sole contribution that universities can make to the education of adults. In recent years there has been a steady increase in the number of refresher or up-dating courses for students already qualified in some particular field and of courses for particular professional groups oriented towards the professional interests of the members. Most of these courses are at high post-graduate level and meet a need not elsewhere satisfied. The development of this kind of provision is something we would wish to see continued and extended to other professional groups, including officials of trades unions. Many participants would welcome some means whereby the successful completion of these courses could be linked with the acquisition of additional recognised professional or academic qualifications. This would be in accord with the concept of continuing education and *we recommend that universities explore means by which such access to additional qualifications might become available. We also recommend that the universities severally or together should explore the possibility of themselves offering certificates or diplomas to mark the successful completion of particular kinds and levels of courses*.

179.   Distinct from their provision for individuals the universities can also make a special contribution to adult education by helping to meet the needs of the community in matters concerned with its general well-being. There are many questions in such fields as social organisation, physical and social environment, economic development, community health and planning which

are increasingly recognised as subjects for informed public discussion. Some of these are highly controversial and may be associated with pronounced differences of interest and strongly-held views. We hope that the adult education service of education authorities and voluntary organisations will encourage the examination of such questions even when they are sensitive. At the same time we realise that there are circumstances in which these agencies for very good reasons might prefer not to become directly involved. An education authority for example might adopt this attitude if there were serious differences of views among the departments of an authority about the questions at issue. In this kind of situation the role of an informed public is very important and universities are well-qualified to promote courses, conferences and seminars to examine the issues in a relatively detached way. In appropriate circumstances they are in a position to offer specialist advice to other educational bodies both statutory and voluntary. Some universities are already in the public interest applying substantial resources to adult education. *We think that, given the expansion we propose, other universities might also be prepared to make a contribution and we recommend that they should be encouraged to do so.*

Staff and Development

180.   Several universities have extra-mural departments with quite substantial numbers of staff engaged full-time on adult education, in others the extra-mural departments are small and some have no extra-mural departments at all. We think that where a university decides to engage in adult education it should have sufficient staff to enable it to carry out its extra-mural role effectively. In this connection we think that more use might be made of the arrangements under the Further Education (Scotland) Regulations 1959, whereby the Scottish Education Department makes grants towards the cost of administrative staff while the education authorities meet the cost of teaching staff in their areas. In addition we consider that grants should be offered by the Scottish Education Department towards the teaching costs involved in special development work and a recommendation to this effect will be made later in this report. The conditions attached to such grants should not be such as to affect the essential academic freedom of the universities or cause difficulties for them in the recruitment or retention of staff.

THE OPEN UNIVERSITY

181.   The Open University is a distinctive form of provision for adults in their leisure time. As such it calls for comment, particularly in regard to the response it has evoked. Hitherto the pattern of demand for enrolment has perhaps been more weighted to professional groups than the originators of the Open University would have wished. It has been sufficiently varied however to illustrate the complexity of the motives which condition the adult's approach to learning. At the same time the Open University's experience has already demonstrated the quite remarkable general response which can be evoked when an institution of higher education by devising original forms of organisation goes far to meet the needs of the individual student.

182.   The contribution the Open University has already made to the application of educational technology to adult learning is outstanding and the adult education service as a whole has much to learn from this experience. Elsewhere

we make more detailed reference to this and also to the relevance of the Open University's experience to our examination of the case for an additional educational TV channel. The extent to which adults who are not enrolled students have chosen independently to follow the broadcast series of the University is a matter for speculation; certainly it was an early hope that many adults would be attracted to do so. The high quality of much of the broadcast material deserves the widest publicity. The adult education service generally has a part to play in attracting adults to the opportunities now available to them through the Open University and in providing guidance in background studies, in selective reading and in other techniques of study which students may eventually require. Participation in some form of adult education as a criterion of willingness to learn is recognised by the Open University in its assessment of applications for admission. In general we see considerable value in the working relationship which the Open University has recognised by securing the representation of adult education organisations within its consultative committees. A similar relationship at local level through the regional organisation of the Open University will have direct practical value for the adult service and for potential Open University students.

183. It is the declared intention of the Open University authorities to try to attract an increasing number of applicants from non-professional and lower-income groups and there is evidence that they are succeeding in doing so. This is in line with our own belief in an expansion of opportunity for all and their aim is one we firmly endorse.

WORKERS' EDUCATIONAL ASSOCIATION

184. The WEA in Scotland is a national voluntary organisation whose sole purpose is to promote and to provide for the education of adults. In its early missionary years its role was to provide working men and women with educational opportunities not then available to them in the State system or denied them by economic circumstances. Today in the field of pre- and post-retirement courses the WEA continues to make a valuable contribution and in this area is seen to be fulfilling the kind of role undertaken by voluntary organisations in pioneering new approaches. Although the Association still continues to offer special services to working people the educational and social developments of the past thirty years have removed many of the inequalities which were the original concern of the Association. The result is that it has become increasingly difficult to distinguish between some of the courses provided by the WEA and some provided by university extra-mural departments, or indeed between the types of students they each attract.

A New Challenge
185. Despite the improvements which have taken place there still exist critical areas in the community where educational needs are not being met. It is in these areas that we think the WEA can be offered the kind of challenge to which it responded in the early years of its existence and which throughout its life has provided a part of its raison d'etre. Responsibility for meeting the educational needs of those adults who by virtue of social, economic, or educational deprivation are less able to articulate their needs or who lack the will or confidence to make use of what is provided rests with the education authority. Concern for the educational needs of this very large group of people

underlies many of our recommendations and in reminding education authorities of this responsibility we are confronting them with a daunting task. But it is the kind of task to the performance of which the energies and resources of a voluntary organisation such as the WEA can most effectively make a contribution. *We recommend that the WEA should make its major contribution the promotion of educational activities appropriate to the needs of the groups described above and that education authorities as part of their comprehensive plan for adult education should seek the help of the WEA in making the relevant provision.*

186.   This area of work which is of the utmost importance to the welfare and development of the community and of society in general is also among the most difficult. The WEA will require time to change the present emphasis of its work and redefine its roles. This would enable practical emphasis to be placed more clearly than before on the WEA's social commitment, thus providing the Association with an opportunity to demonstrate, in the words of one of its former National Chairmen, that the WEA 'is both a social product and a social influence. It registers the social pattern of the age and helps to change it'. This period of readjustment would also provide an opportunity for the Association to explore and assess the problems involved and to try out a variety of approaches on a limited scale on the results of which it might base its plans as it progressively channels its resources into the kind of work we propose.

Financial and other Support
187.   What we have suggested above will be not only difficult but also initially expensive. We hope that education authorities will recognise the importance of the kind of work on which we suggest the WEA should concentrate, will see its relevance in the context of a comprehensive provision of adult education and will support it both financially and by making suitable accommodation free of charge. We recognise however that education authorities' support may not by itself be sufficient and that there will be occasions when the freedom of a voluntary organisation to initiate programmes and activities in its own right could open up entirely new fields and approaches. It is for this reason that we later propose that the scheme of grants from central Government in respect of administrative costs should be continued, and it is open to any WEA district to seek from the Scottish Education Department additional grant towards the cost of employment of additional administrative staff. As has already been indicated, we also propose the introduction of a new scheme of grants, again from central Government, to cover the costs of developmental projects. We hope that the WEA Districts would take full advantage of such a scheme.

Service to Trades Unions and Others
188.   The WEA's original aim to provide educational opportunities for workers has led to a special relationship between the WEA and the trade union movement. We attach much importance to this special relationship and urge continued collaboration with the object of making workers aware of the value of the educational opportunities available to them, extending the range of these opportunities and finding new methods of presenting and developing them. The kind of functions we have already suggested for the WEA and those we now propose in relation to workers in particular are sufficiently similar to suggest that experience in the one will reinforce experience in the other. We

would expect education authorities to support this type of approach which aims to reach the large part of the adult population which until now has been unresponsive to much of educational provision.

189.　So far we have referred to the role of the WEA as that of an agent of the education authorities making a specialist contribution to the overall provision of adult education in a region and this will no doubt absorb much of its resources. In addition however the WEA can also make a valuable contribution to the work of other voluntary organisations and associations. In its evidence to us the Scottish Trades Union Congress described an arrangement of just this kind in which the WEA, operating on a contractual basis, provided educational services of specific interest to the trade union movement. We hope that voluntary organisations generally will make increasing use of this resource.

TRADES UNIONS

190.　The trades unions have a continuing interest in education for reasons which include the fact that the operation of trades unions has become a complicated and highly responsible task requiring knowledge in a great many fields. Shop stewards need more information than ever before in order to perform their functions effectively. Work study, job evaluation and other techniques have to be clearly understood. The widening sphere of trade union interest requires that officials at all levels should be better informed than hitherto about the social and economic framework in which negotiations take place. If the participation of employee representatives in industrial decision-taking is to be effective, there must be a considerable expansion of the quantity and range of educational provision for trade unionists. Responsibility for such training rests with the trades unions themselves but in discharging it they should be encouraged to expand their use of educational agencies. The WEA with its long experience in providing for the education of adults and its close association with the trade union movement seems to be admirably placed to make a valuable contribution to the training of trade union officials and shop stewards. Of equal importance is the involvement of the universities and other institutions of higher education in trade union training in such areas as industrial relations and industrial law. Comparison of the provision of such courses in Scotland and in the industrial centres of other parts of the United Kingdom suggests that more effort and resources should be devoted to such educational activities here. The contrast is particularly marked in the case of day-release courses for trade unionists. There has been only a very limited development of this kind in Scotland, even in those nationalised industries which have encouraged such day-release courses in other parts of the United Kingdom. *We recommend that steps be taken to encourage an extension of the facilities for the training of shop stewards. We consider however that this can be done most effectively only if there is the fullest possible co-operation between universities, colleges of further education and other teaching institutions on the one hand and the trades unions on the other.* Courses should not be offered without prior consultation with the unions concerned on all aspects of their organisation and content. The Trades Union Congress Education Service (Scotland) is the most appropriate point of contact through which the teaching institutions can establish contact with the trade union organisations in regard to the courses being planned and *we recommend that greater use be made of the Service for this purpose.*

Centre for Industrial Relations Training

191. It has been argued that the development of strong regional centres of industrial relations training would greatly assist in the expansion of facilities and especially in the provision of courses tailored for particular groups. We consider that such a centre could play a particularly valuable role in Scotland where the need to expand and develop such training is particularly strong. There is no institution—university or college—which has developed to the point where its experience, expertise and other resources suggest it as an obvious base around which such a centre could develop. Indeed this is a measure of the weakness of the present situation which must be remedied. We are attracted by the proposal made to us by the Scottish Trades Union Congress that a residential adult college be established in Scotland which could specialise in education of interest and value to trade unionists and in particular in industrial relations training, and that such a college should not only run courses for students in residence but be the base from which day-release, in-plant and other courses are organised and provided throughout Scotland (in-plant courses are held within the place of employment of the students). Such a college would meet some part of the need for an expansion of residential facilities as well as the need for a strong regional centre of industrial relations training. It could draw upon the services of existing institutions and organisations active in this field such as universities, colleges and the WEA, and these bodies along with the STUC should be involved in the government of such a centre. The possibility that Robert Owen's New Lanark could provide the location for such a residential centre specialising in educational activities of particular interest to trade unionists would seem eminently appropriate. *We recommend that the possibility of establishing such a residential college and regional centre for industrial relations training be explored by the Scottish Education Department, in consultation with the interested parties.* An exploratory survey carried out on our behalf by the New Lanark Civic Trust Committee suggests that there are at least three existing buildings there which could readily be converted for such a purpose. From talks we have had with the Scottish International Educational Trust we understand that it might be interested in assisting with the establishment and running of such a residential centre.

Participation in Community Education

192. The trade union movement has more than 800,000 members in Scotland, representing a large cross-section of the adult population. We consider it highly desirable that as a part of its concern for the welfare of its members the movement should encourage and promote their involvement in continuing education of a general nature. We commend the Scottish Trades Union Congress for what it has done and is doing in this direction and urge that its activities be continued and expanded. In particular, trades unions and trades councils have much of importance to contribute to the formation and successful operation of a community based educational service for adults and should be encouraged to communicate their views to the education authorities both directly and through active involvement in regional advisory adult education bodies. Additionally the unions should make known to all their members through their network of branches not only the educational opportunities

available to them but also the importance which the trade union movement as a whole attaches to the education of adults.

OTHER VOLUNTARY ASSOCIATIONS

193.   It is relatively easy to identify the educational role of organisations such as the Young Men's and Young Women's Christian Associations, the Scottish Women's Rural Institutes, the National Union of Townswomen's Guilds, the Scottish Association of Young Farmer's Clubs, Co-operative Women's Guilds, community associations and various church-based organisations. There are others however like the Marriage Guidance Council, Councils of Social Service, Family Planning Associations, Consumer Associations, and a host of local organisations concerned with amenity, the arts or sport and recreation, whose educational potential may be obscured by the aims which they explicitly pursue. Their impact on the education of adults is substantial even if considered on the basis of membership alone. In addition to being numerically large their membership includes people of widely varying ages, backgrounds and interests, many of whom may not normally be reached by traditional adult education provision. They provide invaluable points of contact for consumer research into the types, content and duration of courses most likely to attract students and into the most suitable times of the day or the week for classes to be held.

194.   In some of these organisations instruction is given by members who are trained and expert in particular activities. They therefore provide a cadre of instructors for other voluntary organisations or for the statutory authorities. Voluntary organisations have long been pioneers in adult education and many of their ideas and practices have been adopted by the statutory authorities. Encouraging them to continue this pioneering role would be to the benefit of adult education as a whole. We are in no doubt that these organisations can continue to make a valuable contribution to the education of adults in a variety of ways: as initiators of new schemes, as agents for statutory authorities, as advisers on the details of courses and as providers of a large ready-made audience within their membership. It is very desirable that the importance of their role should be more fully recognised both by the voluntary organisations themselves and by the education authorities. The latter should encourage their participation and make their contribution even more effective by providing them with support services when required. Moreover those national voluntary organisations which make a significant contribution to the education of adults and do not at present receive grant aid in respect of it should consider whether they might be eligible for grants towards their administrative costs under the Further Education (Scotland) Regulations 1959. A number already receive such aid but we feel that others should do so to the general advantage of the adult service. *Additionally however we think that voluntary organisations should seek grant aid for developmental projects under our proposed scheme of grants outlined in paragraph 212 and we recommend accordingly.*

SCOTTISH INSTITUTE OF ADULT EDUCATION

195.   We have already described fairly fully the nature and activities of the Scottish Institute of Adult Education (Chapter 3). Unlike the agencies dealt

with above it is not a providing organisation but it must be mentioned here since it plays an important part in the development of adult education and we envisage that it will continue to do so. In paragraph 21 we referred to the lack of a national body charged with the development of adult education comparable to the Consultative Council which operates in respect of the youth and community service; and we indicated that the Scottish Institute had sought to fill this gap to some extent. Earlier in this report we affirm the need for a national council which would advise the Secretary of State and bodies concerned with adult education and generally promote adult education; and we explain why we think it would be inappropriate to charge the Institute with the responsibilities envisaged for such a council. We consider however that the need for the Institute will remain.

196. As the association representative of the academic, statutory and voluntary organisations concerned with adult education in Scotland the Institute has essential functions to perform by providing a channel through which the views of these agencies can be expressed and their interests promoted, by offering a forum for all educationists with special interests in adult education, and by co-operating generally in the further development and extension of adult education. The emergence of comprehensive community education services increases rather than diminishes the need for a body which concentrates on the adult education sectors of these services. Using again the analogy of youth and community service, we would point to the increasing vigour and effectiveness of the Standing Conference of Voluntary Youth Organisations, the association of national voluntary bodies concerned with young people and their needs, since the establishment by the Secretary of State of the Standing Consultative Council on Youth and Community Service. Co-operation and collaboration between the Standing Conference and the Consultative Council has been a major factor in securing the advances which have taken place in the youth and community service and there is every reason to expect similar results from the co-existence of the Institute and the new council we propose. In the new situation arising from the creation of such a council however it would seem necessary for the Institute to reconsider its constitution and functions. *On this basis we recommend that the Scottish Education Department should continue to give financial support to the Institute.*

LIBRARIES, MUSEUMS AND GALLERIES

197. Libraries, museums and galleries are provided by a variety of agencies including central and local government, universities and, particularly in the case of museums and galleries, many private bodies. However their circumstances may differ they all have the same general purpose: to diffuse and increase knowledge. All therefore have an educational function though how an individual institution discharges this function depends on its particular nature and its resources. Together, they represent a vast accumulation of specialist accommodation, staff and other resources particularly suited to adult educational use. Yet despite encouraging experiments and developments in some of these institutions we are firmly of opinion that the great potential for adult education of this rich pool of resources is not being realised under present arrangements. In our view this is a situation which ought to be remedied as soon as possible in the interests of adult education and of the institutions themselves as well as for sound economic reasons. So far as

the institutions are concerned their greater involvement in the adult education system would lead to their use and appreciation by increasing numbers of members of the general public, something which the institutions would certainly welcome. It would also represent a sensible use of valuable resources which are at present being under-used. Since the facilities and resources already exist it would provide a simple and easy way of securing expansion of adult education with minimum delay and at strictly limited additional cost. We now discuss our ideas in more detail.

Libraries

198.   Traditionally the role of the library has been to supply books and information to the reading public and many generations of adult students have reason to appreciate the quality of this service. Many libraries however no longer see this as their sole concern. They now sponsor lectures on a wide range of topics, music recitals, film shows and exhibitions and provide a lending service of pictures, gramophone records, cassettes, films and slides, frequently linked with the lectures, recitals etc. They assist other bodies in matters of publicity, the provision of accommodation, equipment and books and give guidance and instruction on the use of libraries. Many have introduced special provision for particular groups, including the very young and the poorly sighted, and clearly there are opportunities for extension of this kind of special provision to meet the needs of other groups and individuals. We have particularly in mind the house-bound, those in hospital and residential care, those of limited literacy and those in penal establishments.

199.   The public library service therefore already makes a significant contribution to the education of adults but it is capable of increasing its contribution if it is given adequate resources and becomes more closely associated with the education service. In their professional capacity many librarians tend to operate within the confines of their library. They must be encouraged to widen their professional interests and take an even greater part in helping to secure for adults a wider range of educational opportunities. In particular they must ensure that the resources of their libraries are used as extensively and intensively as possible. We think that most libraries are anxious to develop their service in this way, and *we recommend that each library authority should appoint appropriate members of staff to maintain close liaison with those concerned with adult education in their area so that the full resources of the library service may be used in the interests of adult education.*

Museums and Galleries

200.   In 1973 a report* by a Committee appointed by the then Paymaster General to review the needs of the principal local museums and galleries in England, Scotland and Wales and their relationship to the national institutions drew attention to the important contribution which local museums and galleries could make, and some already were making, to education generally. In regard to adult education the Committee referred to the extensive series of evening talks provided by some museums and galleries for adult groups and added '. . . but there is a growing demand for the use of museum facilities by adult education bodies in connection with organised courses. Recent popular television programmes have resulted in an ever-increasing interest in classes in archaeology, local history, art history, antiques and similar subjects. The use of museum premises for organised classes in the evenings or at week-ends

*Provincial Museums and Galleries (HMSO: £1).

is a development which is to be encouraged'. The Committee recommended that education authorities should co-operate closely with museum authorities in planning educational services and that museums should be enabled to provide properly equipped accommodation specifically for educational use. We share these views.

201. The Committee also pointed out that the great majority of local museums and galleries in Scotland have very limited resources. Only 38 of the 90 in Scotland are run by local authorities. In general they tend to operate in isolation and although the Council for Museums in Scotland has done much to promote links with the educational service we think that the closer association of these institutions with a wider system of education for adults, involving universities, public libraries, further education centres, community centres and voluntary organisations, would enable them to extend their services with an assurance of increased public interest and support.

202. We fully appreciate that most local museums and galleries outside the large centres of population do not at present have the staff or other resources to promote an extensive educational service and that even in the larger institutions the staff are frequently hard pressed to maintain the services now provided. We agree with the recommendation of the Committee referred to above that every effort should be made to increase resources and staff and the back-up services available to them. There is much room for improvement in the presentation of their exhibits and the provision of supporting or explanatory material in easily assimilable form. This material should always be available for education purposes, as also should photographs, transparencies, films and tapes. We think there is great scope for the promotion by even the smaller museums and galleries of guided tours, lectures and longer courses in association with the adult education service. The national museums and galleries in Edinburgh and the museums of other large local authorities, particularly those in Glasgow, are developing their educational work and we think they might be very willing to help in providing support services for the educational work of museums in the more thinly populated areas. Touring exhibitions and small mobile exhibitions of pictures and carefully chosen museum objects can be a successful way of bringing a small selection of the resources of museums and galleries to the smaller towns and rural areas and *we recommend that developments of this kind should be encouraged.*

203. We are convinced of the great potential of libraries, museums and galleries for adult education and *we recommend that education authorities should consider with those responsible for the institutions in their areas how their services might be further used on the lines we have suggested. We also recommend that these institutions should be represented on the regional advisory councils which we propose elsewhere in this report.*

LEISURE AND RECREATION DEPARTMENTS

204. It seems likely that responsibility for many of the libraries, museums and galleries referred to above will rest, after the reorganisation of local government, with new committees and departments of leisure and recreation to be set up at regional and district level. These committees and departments are also expected to be involved in provision for indoor and outdoor recreation

through sports centres, parks, playing fields and, in some cases perhaps, community centres. Imprecise though information inevitably is at this stage about the range of their activities, these new committees and departments will be in a position to make significant contributions to community education in its widest sense, and the need is clear for the community education service of education authorities to establish close working relationships with them.

RESIDENTIAL COLLEGES

Short-term Centres

205.   Most of adult education is carried on in the relatively formal atmosphere of the classroom with classes meeting on one night per week for one or two terms. There is a growing tendency to bring groups of adults together in a residential setting for more concentrated periods of study, an arrangement which has obvious advantages. Those involved are removed from their usual routine and provided with facilities more conducive to concentration and reflection. Moreover by being brought into closer contact with others whose beliefs, interests and range of experience may differ from their own they may acquire a greater appreciation of the need for tolerance and understanding. These advantages are widely recognised and accepted and we have already remarked on the number of short-term residential centres now available in other parts of the United Kingdom for this kind of experience. We hope that Scottish education authorities and voluntary agencies will increasingly see the value of this form of adult education and make suitable provision.

206.   Virtually all of the limited number of centres currently available in Scotland provide nothing more than the residential setting. There is little evidence to suggest that any of them have been staffed with the specific object of exploiting the educational value of residence, of ensuring that the additional time provided by residence is used to deepen the experience of the participants rather than simply add to it, or that the experience of living and working together is utilised for the gaining of insight into the participant's own behaviour and that of others. In this respect Scotland lags very far behind England. Newbattle Abbey, the one residential adult college in Scotland, makes provision for short-term work during vacation periods only. A number of education authorities, the extra-mural departments and the WEA run short-term residential summer schools using school hostels, university halls of residence and similar accommodation; but dependence on this type of accommodation imposes severe restrictions as to the potentiality, timing and scale of short-term provision in Scotland. In England alone, on the other hand, there are well in excess of 50 such centres, maintained by local education authorities individually or in consortia, by trusts and by other organisations, offering a wide variety of courses throughout the year. Many are staffed with educationists who either promote courses themselves or offer their skills and knowledge to groups using their centres. We fully recognise that disparity with England does not of itself provide sufficient justification for an expansion of short-term residential provision in Scotland. Careful consideration of the main issues however has led us to the conclusion that provision of this kind is necessary in Scotland and would quickly be justified by public support. *We recommend that the education authorities should give this matter their careful attention and consider the establishment either individually or collectively of a centre or centres, appropriately staffed with short-term residential use in*

mind. We think however that the new region of Strathclyde with its great population could alone support one or more such centres : *and we recommend that the education authority for the region should establish an appropriate number.*

Long-term Centres
207. Newbattle Abbey College has accommodation for some 65 students and provides a two year residential course leading to the College's own Diploma in Liberal Studies. The College has links with adult education agencies through their involvement in its management and because many of its students have come to appreciate the value of education through attendance at adult education evening classes. A residential adult education college linked with other agencies of continuing education is an essential element in provision for those adults who come 'late but in earnest' to education. The College has been and is well supported financially by the Scottish Education Department and by local authorities. *We recommend that this support should be continued with the object of ensuring that the College maintains its special place in adult education in Scotland.* We have considered whether a second long-term residential college for adult education is required in Scotland but have reached the conclusion that judged against Scottish needs alone there is no need for another at the present time. In view of the fact that attendance at long-term residential adult education colleges seems to have little regard to the boundaries between Scotland and England and that the Committee on Adult Education in England and Wales has recommended in their report the establishment of a college in the North of England, we suggest that the Scottish Education Department and the Department of Education and Science should jointly consider whether such a college might be located in the South of Scotland, with the two Departments co-operating in its establishment.

CO-ORDINATION BETWEEN AGENCIES

208. Co-ordination of the work of the many adult education agencies is essential to prevent wasteful duplication, to ensure that existing gaps are filled and to make educational facilities available to all who desire them and would benefit from them. But co-ordination cannot be imposed from without. Ideally it should emerge naturally from the concern of all those involved in the education of adults to give priority to the needs of the community they serve. At present the only forms of consultative machinery available are the extra-mural committees centred on the universities of Aberdeen, Dundee, Glasgow and Edinburgh. (Each of these committees consists of representatives of the university, of the education authorities served by the university in respect of the provision of adult education, of the WEA district and, in one case, of representatives of the central institution and the college of education in the area.) Their main concern is to co-ordinate the provision of academically-based liberal education for adults in the areas of the constituent education authorities and to act as a sounding board for opinion about the kind of courses offered. By the nature of their constitutions their function is important though limited. The major proportion of adult provision is made directly by the education authority and is not therefore their concern. In our view it is now appropriate to establish a new kind of consultative/advisory body with a more extensive remit which would absorb and develop the work of the extra-mural committees. *Accordingly we recommend that regional advisory bodies*

of the kind we describe below should be set up to replace the extra-mural committees.

REGIONAL ADVISORY COUNCILS

209. Within each education authority area a regional advisory council should be established. The exact form that it might take will depend on the area involved. In the larger regions a widely representative body of the kind suggested below is desirable. In the islands authority areas a more simple form of consultative machinery will probably suffice. Whatever form of body is set up however its functions in respect of adult education should include:

(a) keeping under review the provision of community education in the area;

(b) continuing assessment of the adult educational needs of the community as a whole, with particular attention to the needs of the disadvantaged;

(c) identifying particular areas of need in the community and making proposals for appropriate action, including the indication of priorities;

(d) creating and maintaining within the area channels of communication among those involved in the promotion or provision of adult education and the encouragement and maintenance of links with appropriate information centres;

(e) advising on methods of informing the adult public of the educational opportunities available to them.

Regional advisory councils should be broadly representative and should draw on:

(a) organisations in a position to identify community needs—social work departments, councils of social service, youth and community services;

(b) organisations with a 'consumer' interest—voluntary associations, industry, commerce, trades unions, community councils and/or community associations;

(c) organisations with a major concern for providing educational activities —education authorities, university extra-mural departments, WEA Districts, institutions of higher education, such as colleges of education, and other agencies including those with specialist resources of personnel or facilities— sports centres, art centres, libraries and museums.

For effective working we consider that membership should not normally exceed 30 at any time; this suggests that in certain cases there may be a need for some form of rotating membership in order to secure the involvement of all relevant local organisations.

210. Many of the functions we assign to these councils would otherwise have to be carried out by the education authorities themselves if they are to discharge their statutory responsibilities in relation to educational provision for adults. *It therefore seems reasonable that they should be required to take the initiative in setting up the councils within their areas and to assume responsibility for servicing and financing them.*

GRANT AID

211.   At the present the Secretary of State makes grants under the Further Education (Scotland) Regulations 1959 to approved associations engaged in adult education in respect of their costs of administration and *we recommend that this arrangement should continue. The WEA and other voluntary organisations which make a significant contribution to adult education should continue to be regarded as eligible for such grants. We also recommend that the extra-mural departments of those universities presently associated with the extra-mural committees (the replacement of which we recommend in paragraph 208) and others with an active commitment to adult education should be recognised as approved associations for the purpose of receiving grant aid under these Regulations.*

New Scheme of Development Grants

212.   *To enable approved associations to initiate in their own right programmes to meet deficiencies which merit a high degree of priority we recommend that a new scheme of grants should be instituted by the Secretary of State.* Universities with extra-mural departments, other universities which promote a service for adults, and the WEA should be regarded as eligible for grants under the scheme. Any other voluntary organisation which is non-profit making should also be regarded as eligible whether its area of operation is national, regional or local, provided that : (a) the education of adults is among its principal aims and objectives ; (b) it has at least one full-time member of staff a substantial part of whose time is devoted to the promotion of adult education ; and (c) it can satisfy the Secretary of State as to its constitution and fitness to receive grants. These grants should be made in respect of approved developments only. Reference has already been made in paragraphs 101 to 135 to areas of provision which will require development by education authorities, approved associations and voluntary organisations. Particular examples which have been identified are : community development ; adult illiteracy ; the special needs of handicapped adults ; the needs of the elderly, including pre-retirement provision ; education for adult immigrants ; education for parenthood ; and industrial studies. These are the kinds of activities which call for special investigation and development and for which the recommended grants scheme is particularly intended.

213.   The rules governing the scheme should be sufficiently flexible to enable the grants to be either capital or recurrent and to cover all or part of the cost involved. The period of tenure should be clearly stipulated. Applicant bodies should be required to inform the relevant education authority or authorities and the regional advisory council or councils of the submission of any application in order that they might have an opportunity to make representations on the matter to the Secretary of State if they wish to do so. We would expect the relevant education authorities to give maximum co-operation and assistance to those carrying out aided projects and normally to make some contribution towards the cost involved. We suggest that the scheme should operate for a period of, say, seven years in the first instance ; and we propose that the giving of advice to the Secretary of State on the form of the scheme and on applications made under it should be among the functions of a national council whose creation we recommend earlier in this report.

ACCOMMODATION AND OTHER RESOURCES

Use of Schools

214. Although some education authorities make use for adult education purposes of colleges of further education and community centres, and although in the university cities the extra-mural departments have directly under their control accommodation which can be used for teaching purposes, most adult education activity in Scotland has by long established practice taken place in school accommodation. Non-educational accommodation tends to be used only where there is no access to a convenient school. This heavy reliance on school accommodation inevitably imposes severe limitations on the range and quality of the service to adults. The evidence submitted to us has contained frequent reference to the inconvenience and discomfort of meeting in rooms designed and furnished for school pupils and subject to restrictions imposed by the day-time users. We have heard much about the bleak and cheerless classrooms which, despite recent improvements in school accommodation generally, are still in use in many parts of Scotland; about the patient queueing for the solitary sewing machine available for adult use when newer models provided for day school purposes are securely locked away; about the search for space on the roller blackboard where each section is filled with writing conspicuously inscribed 'do not remove'; in short, about a wide range of tensions which can readily and understandably arise when schools are used by different sets of teachers and students. Furthermore since school accommodation cannot normally be used for adult purposes during the day, total dependence on such accommodation results in access to adult education being denied to increasing numbers of adults, eg the shift worker, the young mother and the elderly, for whom day-time attendance is the only practical possibility.

215. Despite limitations of this kind however we recognise that it will be necessary in many areas to continue to use school premises and equipment to a considerable extent and for a long time to come. In addition to the difficulty presented by the lack of suitable alternative accommodation there is a pressing economic need to make maximum use of expensive educational resources. We think it important to stress that school accommodation can be made suitable for adult education purposes at limited costs. In the course of visits members of the Committee saw extremely interesting examples of ways in which conventionally designed secondary schools, available to adults in the evenings only, could be made pleasant, attractive and welcoming to the adult users. This was achieved by straightforward and intelligent attention to the needs of adult education, including all or several of the following every-day details of organisation: well-placed, well-designed information boards showing clearly what courses and classes were on offer; the making available of specialised accommodation and equipment; tea-breaks of 15 minutes or so which allowed members of all the adult classes, varied as they were in age, interests and background, to meet together on a social basis; programmes of educational outings directly linked with courses, well-publicised on the information boards and by duplicated broadsheets; special public presentations of particular subjects or activities, either to test the market or to publicise coming attractions; lively newsletters regularly issued. It is perhaps significant that where such features were found there was almost invariably a full-time adult educationist directing the services of part-time staff. *We recommend that where school accommodation is used for adult education purposes steps*

should be taken to ensure that it is suitable for such use, free from restrictions and attractive to adult students. We also recommend that specialised accommodation should be made freely available for adult purposes.

School-linked Provision

216.   One encouraging innovation in school-building in recent years has been the provision of accommodation purpose-built for non-school users, in the form of a youth, adult or community wing. Accommodation of this kind offers considerable possibilities, particularly that of day-time use, though these have not yet been sufficiently exploited. Too often however such accommodation is underused, being closed at week-ends and for several weeks in the summer, either through lack of staff, lack of enterprise, or as a matter of policy. Another promising development offering the prospect of improved accommodation for adult students has been the move towards 'community schools'. These are planned so that non-school users may share certain facilities with the school and they have certain other accommodation especially designed and set apart for the adults of the community. It is important that the weight of administration of the adult provision and the responsibility for its development should not fall upon the headteacher of the school, although his or her involvement in both is very desirable. School administrative and teaching staff may work in both fields, especially those controlling equipment and facilities, and some staff may be appointed specifically for this purpose; but the appointment of at least one full-time adult educationist is a necessity if the community is of any size.

Community and Adult Education Centres

217.   A similar development is the increasing use of community centres for a variety of adult education activities. These centres have the particular advantage of being purpose-built for adult needs and have the kind of accommodation which allows educational activity to take place alongside the recreational. Members of the Committee visited adult education centres mainly in England, whose sole purpose was to provide for the varied leisure time educational needs of adults. Regrettably there are very few such centres in Scotland. Many of those visited were housed in converted and adapted premises, in disused primary schools for example, but they demonstrated very effectively how, with intelligent attention to lighting, the imaginative use of colour and simple but careful refurnishing, even the most unpromising premises can be converted at limited cost to create an attractive centre for adults. The use of community centres and adult centres, given the right kind of direction and publicity, has the particular merit of attracting adults who might be alienated by a more formal type of centre. *We recommend that community centres and adult centres should be used wherever possible for adult education purposes and that careful attention should be paid to making them attractive to the adult public.*

Libraries, Museums and Galleries

218.   We have already discussed libraries, museums and galleries from the point of view of the specialised contribution they could make to adult education. Many of these institutions however have accommodation suitable for use for more general educational purposes. Increasing use is now being made of suitable museum and gallery space for musical presentations, both recital and appreciation, and this is a development we would wish to see encouraged. As regards the use of library accommodation members of the Committee who

visited Finland were greatly impressed by special accommodation in two branch libraries, one in Helsinki and one in a provincial town. This had been carefully and most effectively planned for use by the music-lending service and also by listening and appreciation groups organised as part of the adult education service. It was regarded as highly successful. Developments of these and similar kinds can add to the amount of attractive accommodation available and enhance the general quality of provision.

Colleges of Further Education

219. Representations have been made to us that the design of the modern college of further education and the range of functions it performs for a wide age group equip it well to play a major part in an expanding service for adults. The relative success which has accompanied greater use of such accommodation under certain education authorities has been noted. The mixing of part-time and full-time users throughout a wide age range helps to create an atmosphere which is likely to attract the adult learner and to make him or her feel more at ease. Because of the variety in length of course it offers, the modes of attendance and the increasing use of block-release arrangements, the organisation of a college of further education has to be able to adjust quickly to changing patterns of demand on its accommodation and may therefore be well able to include some provision for adults. Certain adult studies and activities may indeed be particularly appropriate to a college of further education. *We would recommend that providing authorities should give greater attention than hitherto to the potential for adult education inherent in the colleges of further education, particularly bearing in mind that they are by now well established as centres for adult learning in the vocational context.* This is especially relevant outside the major conurbations since colleges are well spaced geographically over the length and breadth of the country. Adequate administrative staff should be provided. A senior member of the teaching staff, with ready access to the equipment and facilities of the college, might with advantage be appointed to develop adult education in the surrounding area using the college as a base.

General Requirements

220. In any evaluation of accommodation the providers must clearly have regard to the conditions which make for improved learning in the general sense and to those features which are particularly appropriate to adult users of a wide age range. Ease of access, car parking facilities, the adequacy of toilet facilities with provision for the physically disabled, access to cafeteria facilities, the suitability and comfort of seating, and the availability of a variety of rooms including where appropriate rooms with facilities for practical work, are all features which require more attention than they normally receive. It is also essential for centres providing adult education to have ready access to aural and audio-visual equipment and duplicating services. Representation has been made to us from several sources that a lack of storage accommodation is a recurring problem, particularly where the adult service is sharing accommodation or has a form of sub-tenancy. We regard the provision of separate and adequate storage accommodation as essential to the adult service.

221. We do not see the physical provision for the adult education service being made in any uniform way, since circumstances vary considerably even in a relatively small country like Scotland. It is unlikely that even within a

given area there will be exclusive reliance on any single type of accommodation. We are confident that it will be in no sense to the disadvantage of adult users if accommodation with potential for multi-purpose use is appraised on a cost-effective basis. The underlying need at the present time is for *the providers, and particularly the education authorities* as those with the statutory responsibility, to *take careful stock of their resources and accommodation for adults and to develop a strategy for their use and we recommend that they should do so.*

SUPPORT FROM HM INSPECTORATE

222.   Responsibility for the development of education in general including adult education rests with the Secretary of State acting through the Scottish Education Department. HM Inspectorate have access to all the educational establishments which come within the sphere of the Secretary of State. As a result they have a considerable width of view and breadth of experience on which to base the professional advice and judgement they provide for the formulation of national policy. Within the general directives of Government policy they use this knowledge and experience to influence and encourage educational innovation and development and assess the effect of these changes. At present there is a Chief Inspector and six Inspectors whose concern is informal further education which is broadly identifiable with what we have called community education. The widespread nature of community education, involving as it does both statutory and voluntary agencies in its provision and the community as a whole as its consumers, is not reflected either absolutely or relatively in the Inspectorate resources at present allocated to it. The implications for further development inherent in our report will make considerable new demands on HM Inspectorate. We have no doubt that additions to their establishment of a substantial order are necessary if the needs of the expanding service are to be adequately conveyed to the Secretary of State and if the reorganised education authorities are to continue to receive the level of support and encouragement they have now come to expect of HM Inspectorate. Their area of responsibility—informal further education or community education—reflects our own thinking but we would expect that within the establishment a number would have interests and experience specifically in the field of adult education. *We recommend that the number and qualifications of HM Inspectors with responsibilities in this field should be reviewed now in the light of the changes we propose and should be reviewed regularly thereafter.*

11 Staff—Recruitment and Training Etc.

FUNCTIONS

223.   The provision of adult education involves three broad kinds of activities: policy making and administration; organising and stimulating; teaching and discussing. The same individuals may be involved to varying extents in more

than one of these activities and it is very desirable that the three should be closely linked. In particular it is important that those engaged in teaching should be encouraged to contribute to the making of policy and to the stimulation of public interest. The bulk of adult education classes however take place during a very few hours on a limited number of evenings a week and for a limited number of weeks in the year. Courses vary widely in kind and content and the popularity of particular subjects can wax and wane quite rapidly. It would not make economic sense to maintain sufficient full-time teachers to staff so many courses concentrated into such a short period. The great majority of teachers in adult education therefore are and will continue to be employed part-time and appointed for a term or a session, their employment being largely determined by student numbers.

NEED FOR FULL-TIME STAFF

224. The quality of the service will continue to be largely dependent on the skill and enthusiasm of these part-time teachers and if full use is to be made of their qualities and if they are to make the maximum contribution to the work of the service as a whole they must be given proper leadership, guidance and support. For this purpose an adequate full-time staff is necessary with duties which include, as an important element, the planning and organising of courses which will be attractive and valuable not only to students but also to the part-time staff. There is ample evidence from other parts of the United Kingdom and Western Europe that the employment of full-time staff in adequate numbers gives an assurance of sustained effort, progressive planning and flexible and imaginative provision and secures a substantial increase in public support. Our visits furth of Scotland have for example shown us the great value of adult centres staffed with a full-time warden/principal and supporting teaching staff. These centres can be linked with evening centres or other centres staffed on a part-time basis and, with the full-time staff of the adult centre exercising a co-ordinating and guiding function, can be at the centre of a network of provision capable of responding effectively and at the most appropriate time of day to community needs. The value of adult centres with full-time staff does not however lie solely in the increased number of hours they can remain open. It also lies in the commitment of the staff and the quality of their work. In saying this we are by no means undervaluing the work of the many part-time staff who for long have been the mainstay of almost all adult education, but part-time workers no matter how well qualified cannot provide the continuity of interest and expertise that the full-time worker can contribute. Moreover it is reasonable to assume that the employment of full-time staff at all levels in the service will have the effect of encouraging the recruitment of part-time staff and the development of their resources of skill and commitment to the advantage of the service as a whole.

225. In our view, second only to shortage of finance, the main obstacle to extending and improving adult education in Scotland is the shortage of full-time staff. Available information indicates that at present the total number of staff employed full-time specifically in adult education is about 70, including some 30 employed by university extra-mural departments and about 20 by education authorities. Of these nearly half are involved primarily in teaching, about one third in organising and the remainder in administering. In addition, of the 500 or so people employed full-time by education authorities in youth

and community service as organisers, wardens or leaders, there are approximately 60 whose main responsibilities include a substantial amount of work in organising adult education classes. There are thus in Scotland only about 130 people for whom adult education is a major part of their full-time work and only some 90 of these are concerned to a substantial extent with administration or organisation. When these figures are compared with similar figures for other countries on which we have information it is clear that, not only in absolute terms but also in terms of the ratio of full-time to part-time workers, Scotland lags far behind. This poor staffing position has persisted for years in Scotland making it all but impossible to plan comprehensively or to act decisively for the improvement of standards of provision.

ADDITIONAL STAFF REQUIRED

226.   Clearly, substantial improvement is essential if proper attention is to be given to the consideration of long-term policy, the initiation of new forms of education for adults, the stimulation of public interest and demand, the guidance and training of part-time staff and the raising of the general level of organisation and teaching in the service. Simply to give Scotland proportionate equality with England and Wales, without regard to the increases proposed in the Report of the Committee on Adult Education in England and Wales would require an additional 50 full-time appointments in Scotland. If however we are to exploit to the full the wide range of educational resources available in the form of schools, community centres, colleges, universities and their associated staffs, we estimate that a further 100 full-time appointments, making a total of 150 in all, will be required. In addition, the creation of a more favourable ratio of full-time to part-time staff through the provision of adult education centres with full-time heads and supporting teaching staff will require a further 50 full-time workers. If therefore a thriving, responsive and effective service of education for adults is to be established on the basis of our recommendations some 200 additional full-time staff will be required. In our view this requirement can be met over the next five years partly by recruitment from within the ranks of the present part-time workers and partly by attracting young graduates to the service. *We recommend that the Government, the education authorities and the voluntary organisations concerned should adopt this target and give priority to its achievement.*

PRE-REQUISITIES TO RECRUITMENT

227.   There are two main reasons for present staffing inadequacies; the low order of priority in terms of finance and resources accorded adult education by both central and local government; and the absence of any well-established career structure for adult educationists, with promotion opportunities and salary scales capable of attracting and holding staff of the right quality. Adult education is not yet widely recognised as a unified profession embodying a particular ethos and philosophy and with practice based on the principles derived from the study of adult learning. The establishment of career structures linked with common training facilities is an essential pre-requisite for a

determined and sustained drive to secure such recognition and to recruit full-time workers of such quality and in sufficient numbers as will ensure that part-time staff are given the support they need, that attractive and co-ordinated courses can be planned, presented and sustained and a comprehensive service of adult education be provided. *We recommend that the provision of an attractive career structure with opportunities for movement within the wider community service and attractive salary scales should be regarded as matters of the highest priority.*

TRAINING

Present Position

228. Very few of those at present involved either full-time or part-time in our field have received any formal training in adult education though a number have undertaken teacher training courses at various levels. A number of universities in the United Kingdom, including Edinburgh and Glasgow, provide opportunities for training for adult education in the form of courses leading to the award of Certificate or Post Graduate Diploma or M Ed Degree. The numbers engaged in these courses remain consistently small and in Scotland amount to fewer than 30 in a normal year, of whom most are from outside Scotland and of whom only a very small proportion take up full-time employment in adult education in Scotland on completion of training. Opportunities for part-time teachers to obtain training are also extremely limited. They are generally appointed on the strength of their knowledge of their subject whether or not they have had any prior training in teaching skills and are seldom thereafter given an opportunity of taking such training. There is now convincing evidence that what motivates adults to study and the processes by which they learn are sufficiently different from the motivation and learning of children to justify special training for those who will be concerned either as teachers or as organisers with the education of adults. There is thus no logic in the current situation in which training is regarded as essential for teachers in primary, secondary and vocational further education but not for those engaged in teaching in adult education. The expanded and efficient service we wish to see in Scotland can be achieved only by staff whose personal qualities are matched by the relevance and thoroughness of their training.

Need for Thorough Review

229. As the service grows and the scope of its activities expands the range of skills required will multiply and the need to use these skills with maximum efficiency will become progressively more important. This will give rise to many problems in training. The diversity of the service involves a wide variety of providers, including education authorities, industry, the universities, and many voluntary organisations, and this will make it difficult to devise training arrangements which meet all their various circumstances and needs. In this situation there is a need for a thorough examination of training provision generally recognising the following broad principles:

(a)   a sense of common purpose must be developed as a means of en-couraging maximum co-operation and eliminating competition or wasteful duplication of effort; and to ensure this all those engaged in the work must be enabled to understand the functions and aims of the others;

(b)   training for each of the several sectors of this wider community field should not be carried out in isolation; and

(c)   the common core of knowledge and expertise concerned with adult education should be included within the training schemes for each of these other sectors.

Review by Scottish Council

230.   *We recommend that* as the concept of a comprehensive community education service becomes more fully reflected in practice in the field *the professional training needs of the service and of the several branches of it should be reviewed at regular intervals by the Scottish Council for Community Education* (see para 165).

Training of Full-time Staff

231.   In the short term we are concerned with the recruitment and training of the 200 additional full-time staff needed over the next five to seven years. Although some of these will be needed as full-time teachers of adults, eg to staff the proposed adult centres, the majority will be concerned with the promotion, co-ordination, and administration of adult education and with the training of part-time workers, which requires skills of a high order. *We recommend that all seeking a career in adult education, whether their initial preference is to teach or to organise, should undertake an appropriate course of training.* As far as possible the pattern of training should meet individual interests and preferences through a series of options; but it should nevertheless have common elements so that those who have undertaken training should be able to operate in a variety of situations in the wider community field. When more specialised training is needed employing agencies should promote it on an in-service basis.

232.   We think that such expansion could be secured without undue difficulty in view of the fact that the pattern for training of this kind has already been established in the Diploma in Adult Education courses offered by the Universities of Edinburgh and Glasgow where staff with the necessary specialised knowledge and experience in relevant fields are already available. In addition the colleges of education have considerable experience and expertise in the training of teachers and two of them, Moray House and Jordanhill, have many years of experience in the training of youth and community service workers. *We therefore recommend that the Diploma in Adult Education courses at the Universities of Edinburgh and Glasgow should be expanded and developed as a first and urgent priority* and that these Universities and Colleges of Education should co-operate in making the necessary provision in the same way as they already co-operate in the Bachelor of Education degree courses. Should there be a substantial increase in the demand for training at this level consideration should be given to the development of similar joint courses at other Scottish universities and colleges of education. We have noted with satisfaction that these Diploma courses are available on a part-time (two-years) as well as a full-time (one-year) basis, a flexible arrangement which should facilitate recruitment. At present the normal qualification for entry to them is possession of a first degree or equivalent but in practice both Universities have interpreted this requirement liberally and have admitted candidates qualified in other ways, without reduction in course standards. It is important that this flexibility on entrance to these courses should be maintained.

Eligibility for Students Allowances

233. Awards under the Students' Allowances Scheme are granted by the Scottish Education Department to eligible students attending full-time first degree courses at universities and comparable courses at other establishments of further education. As an extension of this scheme and subject to certain conditions, awards may be continued in respect of a post-graduate course of vocational training, teacher training for instance, provided that this is necessary for admission to a first and basic career. Until 1973 awards under the foregoing Scheme were not available for the post-graduate courses leading to the Diploma in Adult Education at the Universities of Edinburgh and Glasgow on the ground that these Diplomas were not recognised professional qualifications. Following enquiries made on our behalf however it was agreed that such courses should be regarded as eligible with the reservation that this decision should be regarded as a temporary one pending further investigation of the position. In the circumstances we feel it necessary to record our belief that it is of great importance to the future of the adult service that there should be employed within it persons of high quality and attainment and accordingly that suitably qualified persons wishing to enter these post-graduate courses should not be prevented from doing so by an inability to secure necessary financial support. *We strongly recommend that these courses should continue to qualify for grants under the provisions of the Students' Allowances Scheme.*

In-Service Training

234. Following initial training opportunities should be provided for the acquisition of specialist knowledge and for the updating of administrative and teaching skills. Adult educationists should be made more aware of the relationships between their skills and those applied in formal education, the Open University, or industrial retraining. This might best be achieved by joint training undertaken in a residential setting and arrangements for such in-service training should be introduced as soon as possible. *We recommend that the universities and colleges of education should co-operate jointly and with employing bodies in this provision.*

Adult Education as a Constituent of other Professional Training

235. Elements in the courses provided for those preparing for posts in adult education should also be made available to those undergoing training for certain other professions. The overlapping functions of adult educationists and youth and community workers should be reflected in course elements which are common to the training of both groups. Courses for intending social workers could benefit from the inclusion of training in the skills of communication and intending adult educationists should be offered elements in the training for social work. In addition to the acquisition of appropriate skills such common elements in training could prove helpful in developing a more unified approach to the personal and social problems requiring help from these different services. *We recommend that these views should be drawn to the attention of the appropriate training authorities.*

236. *We recommend that the universities and colleges of education should consider the inclusion of adult education as an option in the initial training courses for teachers and at special subject level in at least some of the present Bachelor of Education degree structures operated by colleges of education.* This would provide a useful introductory training for those wishing

to undertake work in adult education on a part-time basis and would also help to build up a cadre of trained teachers and administrators well qualified to make an effective contribution to the growing concept of school-based community education. *We also recommend that, as the importance of adult education within community education becomes more fully recognised, every Bachelor of Education course should include an appreciation of the purpose, characteristics and problems of adult education.* Once education is recognised as a continuing process, with education in school leading on to a wide range of educational opportunities and experiences in later life, a teacher who lacked knowledge of adult education would be considered ill-equipped to function effectively in the other segments of the educational continuum.

Training of Part-time Staff

237.   The formulation of proposals for the training of part-time teachers presents special difficulties. Most are engaged in other employments which have prior claims on their time. Particularly in rural areas, many might find it inconvenient to attend centralised training courses. But such a large proportion of the teaching in adult education is carried out by part-time staff that it seems to us that any action designed to improve their competence in the art of teaching adults as distinct from their knowledge of their particular subjects must have an important beneficial effect on the service as a whole and must therefore be encouraged. In addition we think that the fact of having devoted himself to the task of acquiring such training and the consciousness thereafter of being a trained adult educationist would be likely to create within the individual a sense of professionalism and commitment and therefore help to reduce the persistently high rate of turnover of part-time staff. *We recommend that education authorities should be required to make available, as soon as is practicable, adequate and efficient training facilities for part-time workers in adult education, particularly for those entering the service for the first time.* The major responsibility for the provision of such training should rest with the education authorities in co-operation, according to the particular subject content, with the university extra-mural departments, colleges of education, and other colleges. In the case of the larger regions we would strongly urge that consideration be given to the appointment of a full-time training officer in order to facilitate maximum co-ordination.

238.   It would be unrealistic however to expect either newcomers or existing part-time staff to undertake such training in satisfactory numbers without some incentive. Certain education authorities in Scotland and some in other parts of the United Kingdom operate arrangements under which part-time staff who have satisfactorily completed a course of training are paid at higher rates than those who have not. This not only provides a reward for undergoing training but also serves as an inducement to the teachers concerned to enter into a commitment to adult education and continuity of service in it. *We recommend that the principle of incentive payments related to training should be extended within Scotland.*

239.   An administrative pattern for the organisation of such courses already exists in Scotland in the training for both voluntary and part-time paid youth and community workers. Many of these courses operate at regional level, providing not only general background but also special activity training to a fairly high level. Consideration should be given to the inclusion within such training of appropriate modules of adult education. This would provide

further opportunities for increasing understanding and co-operation between the complementary parts of an expanded community education service.

FEES AND EXPENSES OF PART-TIME TEACHERS

240. The general level of fees payable to part-time tutors is too low having regard to the value of the services they provide and to the need to attract persons of high qualifications and attainments in numbers adequate for the expanded service we recommend. There has been a tendency for these fees to lag behind movements in professional salaries generally and the effect of this has been accentuated by the high rates of taxation often levied on the additional earnings of some part-time tutors. There is clear evidence that these factors have deterred many who would otherwise have been fully prepared to undertake part-time work in adult education. An interesting consequence of the heavy incidence of taxation on marginal additions to earnings from part-time teaching is that the net cost to the public purse of any additional expenditure on part-time teaching is substantially lower than the cost of fees paid. This vitally important issue of the remuneration of part-time tutors must be examined and improvements introduced if the service is to develop and expand as we have proposed.

241. Under present arrangements education authorities have complete discretion in regard to the fees and the travelling and subsistence allowances they pay to part-time tutors. As regards fees, a committee of education authorities agreed general rules with the intention that they should be adopted by all. However these rules have no statutory force and not all education authorities at present apply them. A situation of this kind can give rise to anomalies and create dissatisfaction. A tutor employed by more than one education authority may in fact receive different fees for the same kind of work. The position in regard to travelling and subsistence allowances is similar and there are other sources of dissatisfaction in the present arrangements. Teachers often have to travel considerable distances from their homes to the centre in which they teach and for many of these journeys public transport facilities are unacceptably time-consuming or simply non-existent. Yet those who provide their own transport may receive travelling allowances which fail to meet the actual cost and may receive no adequate allowance to compensate for the time spent on the journey. Teachers naturally prefer engagements which involve minimum travelling time with the result that many outlying areas experience staffing difficulties.

242. *We recommend that steps should be taken to encourage all education authorities to co-operate in devising and implementing improved scales of fees for part-time teachers in adult education* which adequately recognise the qualifications of the teachers and the nature of the work being undertaken. *We also recommend that joint action of this kind should be taken in regard to travelling and subsistence allowances* which take account of the travelling time involved. We would emphasise that our concern is not only to raise the general level of remuneration but also to eliminate existing anomalies. This should be possible by agreement between the education authorities themselves with guidance from the national council which we earlier recommended should be established. Should agreement not be reached in this way we would

recommend the introduction of statutory scales for general application with adequate safeguards for rural and isolated areas.

12 Other Matters

STUDENT FEES

243.   At present education authorities have complete discretion as to the level of fees charged to students for adult education courses provided by them or by other bodies acting on their behalf; and their practices vary. It has been put to us in evidence that fees for such courses should be abolished, that they act as a disincentive to recruitment, keeping out many of those who might be expected to benefit most from participation, that primary and secondary education are provided free and that in equity adult education should also be provided free; and that the cost of abolition would not be as great as might be feared since it would be offset by savings on the cost of assessment and collection.

244.   We have examined these arguments with care but do not find them convincing. There is as yet no firm evidence to support the view that fees act as a deterrent or that their abolition would bring about substantial advantages. The comparison with primary and secondary education is not a valid one since it leaves out of account the compulsion under statute to engage in primary and secondary education, at least up to the age of 16, and the fact that these are full-time activities as opposed to the voluntary part-time nature of adult education. While abolition would save the cost of assessment and collection there would undoubtedly be a net loss of income and a corresponding reduction in the amount available for development of the service.

245.   In our view the charging of a fee brings positive advantage. It helps to establish the strength of interest in particular subjects and thus enables the providing body to plan its programme in such a way as to make the most effective use of its resources. It also exerts a certain discipline on the student to continue the activity of his choice rather than waste his money, while by paying a fee he acquires the status of a paying customer with a right to a say in the kind of service provided. On the other hand, the abolition of fees by removing the sanction which discourages students from entering courses capriciously would hinder rather than assist comprehensive planning which depends on reasonably reliable indications of the strength of student interest and on continuing student support.

246.   We do not accept that it is in any way unreasonable to expect the average adult to make a contribution towards the public cost of facilities designed to help him make purposeful use of his leisure time. *We therefore recommend that the present general practice of charging fees for adult education classes and courses should not be discontinued*. But we see it as necessary to create a fee structure, which will assist the development and expansion of the service by securing a reasonable contribution from the participants as a whole and at the same time allow special arrangements to be made for those whose participation is highly desirable in their own and the community's interest but

who without such arrangements might not be able to take full advantage of the opportunities available.

An English Arrangement

247.   The fee arrangements operated by certain local education authorities in England have been designed to meet these points. They provide that, for fee purposes, courses should be divided into two categories, (a) 'aided' and (b) 'economic'. An aided course is a progressive educational course which may run for any period up to three years and which is open to any student who has so far spent less time on a particular course than the full period required for the course as advertised. The fee charged is a nominal one and there is special provision for reduction or waiving for particular groups, such as the elderly and the disabled. The fee income does not cover the cost of providing the course and subsidy is therefore required. An economic course on the other hand requires a fee income sufficient to meet the teaching costs. The smaller the number of enrolments the larger the fee; the larger the number the lower the fee; but the fee is never reduced to a lower figure than the aided course fee whatever the number of enrolments.

248.   There are two kinds of economic courses:

i   those for students who (either as a result of having already completed an aided course or otherwise) have already studied the relevant subject to the highest level which an aided course in the centre concerned can offer and wish to pursue their interests in the subject purely as a recreation; and

ii   those of a mainly recreative kind which are similar to courses which might be followed privately (golf instruction, for example) or which might popularly be regarded as luxuries.

The provision of an economic course does not depend on a specified minimum number of students but does depend upon the students who wish to join such a class from the beginning being willing to pay a fee determined by dividing their number into the economic cost of the class. There is a firm guarantee that such a course once started will not be discontinued even if the attendance falls. Experience has shown that despite their relatively high fees economic courses generally attract increasing numbers of students.

249.   An arrangement such as this has a good deal to commend it. Without reducing unacceptably the total income from fees it enables relatively low fees to be charged to new students taking up a subject for the first time and to students of limited means. By enabling the teaching costs of certain courses to be met in full it makes more public money available for desirable courses which might not otherwise be provided and also for experiment and innovation. The arrangement is therefore worthy of consideration by Scottish education authorities. However there are certain inherent difficulties. Some courses will not fall clearly into either the aided or the economic category and quite arbitrary decision may have to be made. There is difficulty too in determining whether the motives of a student in embarking on the study of a particular subject are mainly recreational or otherwise and equal difficulty in being precise about the nature of the benefits he will eventually obtain from his pursuit of it. A danger to be guarded against is that of favouring those who are prepared to join courses in the traditional academic subjects and of creating a further deterrent to those who need to be wooed back to education by a non-academic approach based on their recreational interests.

A Scottish Arrangement

250. An arrangement operated by a Scottish education authority provides maximum flexibility in regard to minimum numbers and at the same time allows a considerable degree of student involvement. A voluntary association or a centre acting as a voluntary association is charged a block fee for each teacher or instructor provided. The individual class fees are determined by the members of the centre or the association, the only proviso being that the total of the block fees must be recovered. Clearly such a system can operate only where individual class members or their representatives are enabled to meet as a group and participate in making decisions about the programme to be provided. Reduced block fees are charged if the provision is designed to open up new ground or if a substantial number of senior citizens are involved. Thus large classes in a popular subject can subsidise smaller classes so reducing the risk of the latter failing to start or of being discontinued if numbers fall below an arbitrary figure.

251. We think that such arrangements might with advantage be applied to any organised groups with a particular subject interest who seek a course specially designed to meet their own requirements and to which admission is confined to their own membership. We would expect any such arrangement to require from the special groups a fee sufficient to meet at least the teaching costs. This would give to the consumer the provision he wants at a cost which is to a certain extent within his control, since the cost per student will depend on the numbers in attendance. At the same time it would enable the providers to discharge some of their responsibilities at limited cost, freeing more resources for more basic provision and for development activities. As a further variant we should like to see some account being taken of what the market is willing to bear, ie that more might be charged for a popular course in order that a lower fee might be charged for one which is less popular but nonetheless important, or in order to support experimental work.

252. Consideration should also be given to the social needs of particular areas with a record of non-participation in adult education, and very low fees charged in such areas. Moreover, we think that fees should always be waived for young people in the 16–18 age group, whether at school or in employment, for people over the normal pension age (65 for men and 60 for women) and for the disadvantaged (see paragraph 108) whether attending open courses or restricted courses specially designed for them.

253. *We therefore recommend that the future fee structure should be sufficiently flexible to encourage the expansion of the service as a whole, the development of new kinds of courses, and the involvement of more students and a wider range of students. It should provide for the needs of special groups and particular areas, including rural areas, and for the waiving or remission of fees for individuals or groups in appropriate circumstances.*

CLASS SIZES

254. Under present arrangements most education authorities in Scotland will not provide a course unless there is a stipulated minimum number of enrolments for it; and further a course once started may be discontinued at any time if the number of students in attendance falls below another stipulated figure. The

imposition of such conditions is not based on any statutory requirements. On the contrary education authorities have been given complete discretion in the matter of the provision or continuance of classes and it is in the exercise of this discretion that these minimum requirements are imposed. Since individual education authorities generally operate independently of one another in the matter the arrangements vary from one area to another. We recognise that arrangements of this kind are necessary to ensure the best use of available resources but too rigid an application of them carries a risk that the needs of many minority groups will not be met and the opportunities for experimentation and innovation which are regarded as essential to a proper development of the service will be unduly limited. Our investigations suggest that these dangers have not been entirely avoided. Limitations of staff and other resources make it impossible for every request for adult provision to be met but the rules as presently applied undoubtedly have the effect of preventing the provision of some minority interest courses which can probably never be expected to attract more than very small numbers; and the success or failure of a course cannot be judged simply by reference to student numbers. An education authority cannot be regarded as having properly discharged its duty to secure an adequate and efficient service throughout its area until it has explored all alternative ways of meeting expressed needs. It should be seen to be as much the duty of an education authority to stimulate and encourage the interest of members of the public in courses which may be less popular than others as to concentrate on those of established popularity. Lack of interest in a subject may be no more than lack of knowledge of it and given the right kind of encouragement and opportunity the low popularity course of today could in some instances become the very popular one of tomorrow.

255. *We therefore recommend that education authorities should be sympathetic to and understanding of the position of minority interest groups in determining their policies relating to the provision and continuance of classes.* Where difficult circumstances arise we suggest that in exploring the alternative ways in which they might discharge their duties they should consider, for example, the provision of transport, the use of the Open University, the provision of correspondence courses, the supply of tapes, cassettes etc. Where none of these alternatives meets the circumstances they should be particularly flexible in applying their regulations as to class sizes.

PAID LEAVE FOR ATTENDANCE AT ADULT EDUCATION CLASSES

256. Our investigations have shown that except in the case of a very small number of persons attending classes in preparation for retirement and, as a result of initiative taken by the Standing Consultative Council on Youth and Community Service, of voluntary youth leaders attending training courses and camps, paid leave for the purpose of attendance at classes which have no direct vocational purpose is virtually unknown in Scotland today. This is perhaps not surprising considering that the principle of day and block release even for vocational further education purposes receives only limited support in Scotland and less than in most other parts of the United Kingdom. Yet few employers would argue against the proposition that to provide workers with opportunities for improving their general educational standards

and developing outside interests would be of value to these workers not only as individuals but also as employees and therefore of some value to the employers and to the wider society.

257.   There is general recognition of the fact that the highly industrialised society of today imposes on employees stresses and strains which are major causes of ill health and that a large number of working days are lost each year as a direct result. Many of the larger and more enlightened employers provide physical recreational facilities like bowling greens and tennis courts to help counter the effects of these stresses and to enable their employees to develop wider recreational interests. Some grant paid leave to employees to engage in physical recreational activities. Yet few make any kind of provision for those of their employees whose recreational interests lie not in these fields but rather in the direction of the study of a language or a craft. We think the time has come for more employers to recognise the value of this form of recreational activity and for them, encouraged and assisted by central Government, the education authorities and voluntary organisations, to provide opportunities for their employees to engage in it.

258.   Such activity can take various forms and may involve time away from work; and there may therefore be wide differences in the time and costs involved. Where the numbers employed are large provision may be 'in-plant' and the time lost from work thus kept to a minimum. In smaller establishments or where the educational interest of the employee is highly specialised time-off may also be required to travel to where the appropriate class is available. With the development of paid educational leave it is to be expected that a variety of class subjects will be made available in educational centres in towns and cities. The educational potentialities and needs of some employees will justify their release from employment for longer periods than are required to attend a weekly class; some will require regular day-release and the needs of others may be best served by attendance at a short residential course.

259.   We consider that the practice of granting paid leave to enable employees to attend educational courses should be encouraged. The arrangements and conditions under which such leave might be granted and the times when it might be taken would be matters for agreement between the employer and the individual employee and would need to have regard to the manning requirements of the firm concerned. An employee applying for such leave would have to show evidence of having engaged in serious and systematic study on a leisure time basis or of having been prevented from so doing by exceptional circumstances.

260.   We recognise that in this matter the support of employers is of critical importance and we think that central Government should offer some induce-ment to employers to give such support. In this connection we have examined the Report of the International Labour Conference, 58th Session, 1973. It reports on a questionnaire on the subject of paid educational leave which was sent to the governments of State Members of the International Labour Organisation. Question No 26 in the questionnaire asked for 'Other suggestions regarding measures for promotion of paid educational leave?' The substance of the reply given by the United Kingdom Government is reported as 'There might be a place for suggested incentives to employers to grant paid educa-tional leave'. *Accordingly we recommend that a scheme of incentives to*

employers who grant paid leave to their employees for the purpose of attend-
ance at adult education classes and courses should be introduced by Her
Majesty's Government.

STUDENT PARTICIPATION

261.   As the service develops we would hope that students would be encouraged to play a part in the administration of the centre they attend. For
example, we would hope to see them involved in matters relating to programmes, including the preparation of the list of courses to be offered at the
start of a session, any subsequent changes in the approved programme,
proposals for the termination of any course and the way in which the resources
of the centre are used. Arrangements of this kind would foster a friendly and
co-operative relationship between the centre, its staff and the students and
thus help to strengthen student commitment to adult education. We think
it desirable that *whenever the number of students in a centre makes it practi-*
cable to do so there should be appointed, under the chairmanship of the head
of the centre, a management council of the kind provided for in terms of
Section 125(3)(d) of the Local Government (Scotland) Act 1973, which
includes representatives of both staff and students; and we recommend
accordingly. The responsibilities to be given to such councils should include
responsibilities in relation to the matters referred to above.

262.   *We also recommend, where student numbers make it practicable the*
setting up by election of a Students' Association with power to appoint
representatives to the Management Council mentioned above. Such an
association might also undertake responsibility for arranging social activities
of all kinds.

FINANCIAL ASSISTANCE TO STUDENTS

263.   We have already referred (paragraphs 232 and 233) to the post-graduate
courses leading to the Diploma in Adult Education at the Universities of
Edinburgh and Glasgow and to the importance we attach to their continued
recognition for the purposes of the Students' Allowances Scheme operated
by the Scottish Education Department. In addition however education
authorities have discretionary power under the Education (Scotland) Acts
which enable them to grant bursaries to persons ordinarily resident in their
area for attendance at part-time and non-advanced full-time courses of further
education. Many courses of importance to adult education fall within this
category including for example courses for part-time teachers of adults,
short-term residential courses and longer-term residential courses of the
kind offered at Newbattle Abbey College.

264.   So far as adult education courses are concerned education authorities
at present make very little use of these discretionary powers. As a result
many adult students are unable to take full advantage of provision available
to them because they are unable to meet the relevant costs. This is especially
true where residence is involved. Elsewhere we have discussed the value of
residential education and suggested that for many adult students, particularly
those seeking a second chance to proceed to higher education after what in

many cases will be years of absence from study, it offers almost the only chance of success. But it is also true of other situations not involving residence. Our attention has been drawn to the fact that a number of adult students, many of them housewives, have enrolled as non-graduating students in universities taking one or sometimes two classes and generally with marked success. Their motives are entirely educational—they wish to follow an interest in a chosen subject and to test themselves at university level. Many of them would probably have preferred to attend a full-time course of study—for which they might have been eligible for an award under the Students' Allowances Scheme—but were prevented from doing so by domestic or other circumstances. They have not been able to secure assistance from education authorities for their part-time course and must therefore themselves pay the fee amounting to some £45. Only those in a position to pay this sum are therefore able to attend. There is evidence to suggest that others would enrol if they could afford to do so.

265. Similarly we think that there is a need for education authorities to show a greater willingness than at present to provide assistance to students in relation to fees for Open University courses. We have been given to understand that in the absence of such assistance many students have found it impossible to take advantage of the opportunities provided by the Open University.

266. *We therefore recommend that steps should be taken to encourage education authorities to make more extensive use than at present of their discretionary powers to give assistance to adult students for courses of all kinds and particularly for those involving periods of residence.*

13 Cost of Implementing Recommendations

267. The inadequacy of available statistical information and in particular the absence of comprehensive information about expenditure on the provision of adult education makes it impossible for us to estimate the additional cost of implementing the programme of expansion we recommend. Some of the proposed expansion is experimental requiring special attention from organisers and teachers, and therefore likely to involve higher than present average costs. On the other hand, the integration of the youth and community service with adult education could be expected to lead to economies of scale and the possibility of some expansion at less than present average costs. These are matters which require more specialist attention than we have been able to give to them. Moreover, the cost of some of our major recommendations would require to be shared between various branches of the education service. This would apply, for example, to our recommendation on the future use of broadcasting for educational purposes.

268. Central to our recommendations for general expansion are those we make for the creation of a larger body of appropriately trained professional staff working with larger numbers of part-time teachers for whom training facilities are available; and we have tried to estimate the cost of implementing

these particular recommendations on the basis that the additional full-time staff will require to be appointed over the next five years and the expansion achieved by the mid-1980s by which time the additional part-time staff would also be in post.

269. We estimate that from the mid-1980s onward the annual cost in salaries and fees of the additional full-time and part-time staff required, together with supplementary travel and related costs and the cost of the necessary training programme might amount to about £1m at 1974 costs. In addition there would be the once-for-all training costs involved in the expansion of full-time staff by 200 over five years which we estimate at about £350,000 ie £70,000 per annum.

270. We feel it necessary to emphasise that these estimates do no more than give a broad and tentative picture of the order of magnitude of one major element of the costs of the expansion we recommend. Experience suggests that such salary and related costs will represent something of the order of 50 per cent of the total expenditure involved. Perhaps the most notable point about this estimate is how small it is in relation to total public expenditure on all forms of school, further and higher education in Scotland, which was approximately £400m in 1972–73.

Addendum

NOTE OF DISSENT BY MR M T SWEENEY

It is with some regret that I find myself out of step with the hopes, proposals and recommendations of the Alexander Committee on the question of the Workers' Educational Association.

The Report states, 'We hope that education authorities will recognise the importance of the kind of work on which we suggest the WEA should concentrate, will see its relevance in the context of a comprehensive provision of adult education, and will support it both financially and by making suitable accommodation free of charge. We recognise however that education authorities' support may not by itself be sufficient and that there will be occasions when the freedom of a voluntary organisation to initiate programmes and activities in its own right could open up entirely new fields and approaches. It is for this reason that we later propose that the scheme of grants from central Government in respect of administrative costs should be continued, and it is open to any WEA District to seek from the Scottish Education Department additional grant towards the cost of employment of additional administrative staff. As has already been indicated, we also propose the introduction of a new scheme of grants, again from central Government, to cover the costs of developmental projects'.

I base my dissent upon my experience with the WEA in Scotland as a customer, a competitor and up to now as a co-operator; by my assessment of some of the evidence relevant to Scotland and the statistical evidence available.

When I was first approached to serve on the Alexander Committee I refused. Later I was approached again and it was pointed out that my long involvement with adult education through the WEA, the National Council of Labour Colleges (NCLC) and since 1964 with the TUC Education Service in Scotland was a very weighty experience and should be added to the deliberations of this Committee, and so I came to serve.

On the Committee I found that my background, education and experience was so different from many of my colleagues that I am pleasantly surprised that we agreed about so many of the findings of the Committee. However, as far as the WEA in Scotland is concerned I feel that the conclusions arrived at are wrong and that I must honestly try to say why I think they are wrong.

For about half of the time the WEA has been operating in Scotland I have been close to it in various capacities. First as a humble *customer*—student, WEA Branch Officer, delegate to a district committee and as an acting unpaid organiser with some degree of success.

Secondly when in 1953 I became the Tutor/Organiser of the National Council of Labour Colleges (NCLC) in the West of Scotland. We were engaged in teaching 'independent working class education' (EDUCATION FOR CHANGE) and in this area I was a friendly *competitor* of the WEA for trade unionists and other worker students. I helped the WEA District Secretary on numerous occasions.

The third phase of my 'closeness' to the WEA was as a *co-operator*. In 1964 as a result of agitation within the trade union and labour movement to rationalise working-class education, the British Trades Union Congress took over a part of the WEA, the Workers' Education Trade Union Committee (WETUC), and along with the Postal Courses Section of Ruskin College and the NCLC formed the TRADES UNION CONGRESS Education Service; and I became the regional officer for this service in Scotland.

Two great opportunities were afforded to the WEA at this time. First of all it was invited to play a major part in the provisions to be made by the TUC Education Service in Scotland. The TUC set aside the sum of £30,000 to be paid to the WEA centrally, of which £3,000 was for administrative costs, the rest to be drawn upon for use in providing schools, classes and courses approved by the TUC in London. The WEA was thus provided with an opportunity to operate through the trade unions to publicise and promote itself as an educational body. For the first two or three years the WEA in Scotland was pretty enthusiastic about this opportunity and in the first full year of this co-operation they produced the following figures of trade union students.

Year I (1965/6)

	No. planned	No. cancelled	No. actually held	No. of students
Linked Weekend courses	19	Nil	19	379
Single Weekend „	17	2	17	307
Linked Day „	26	13	13	301
Single Day „	13	6	7	148
Evening „	13	12	1	9
	88	33	57	1,144

Compare this with the up-to-date situation.

Year 9 (1973/4)

	No. planned	No. cancelled	No. actually held	No. of students
Linked Weekend courses	0	0	0	0
Single Weekend „	13	7	8	120
Linked Day „	0	0	0	0
Single Day „	0	0	0	0
Evening „	0	0	0	0
	13	7	8	120

The second opportunity afforded the WEA in Scotland also occurred in 1964. It arose from a TUC decision to narrow down the range of subjects to be taught in their courses and to insist that these were to be provided only for members of trade unions. This excluded thousands of former NCLC students who were not trade unionists and who should have been attracted to the more aptly named Workers' Educational Association. The WEA failed to gather in these people. Two fine opportunities were therefore missed.

I do not think the WEA is capable of re-establishing its former position in trade union education or of selling its ordinary general education classes to many trade unionists. Growing numbers of trade unions now carry out their own educational work and seldom call in the WEA to run internal union courses for them; this is equally true of the STUC. The TUC Education Service in Scotland has to turn away many weekend course students because of shortage of money and other resources and although the WEA is still a partner in our Service in Scotland, the statistics for 1973/74 show that its influence is dwindling. The WEA delegation to the Alexander Committee when giving evidence orally claimed to be involved in the provision of more and more classes for the labourer/docker/bus driver type of person than ever before. This may be true with reference to England and Wales but no such classes appear in the trade union WEA statistics for Scotland.

In the field of liberal adult education in general the part played by the WEA is a modest one. Figures for class enrolments for the year 1972/73 show that out of a total student enrolment for classes in Scotland of 217,000 the WEA was credited with providing 4,000; and doubt has been expressed as to whether or not a proportion of these figures were 'duplicated' in that they were counted also by some other body. The 4,000 is less than 2 per cent of the total.

One important organisation whose members have close working connections with the WEA ie, The Association of Directors of Education in Scotland, gave both written and oral evidence to the Committee. In paragraph 6 of page 4 of their written evidence they stated in forthright language:

'The Workers' Educational Association in Scotland is a transplant from an entirely different set of conditions in England and Wales. Despite the hard work of its officials and the enthusiasm of its few key members our Association have to conclude reluctantly that the WEA in Scotland are making little or no contribution to the initiation of new classes or activities or to increasing class attendance by adults.'

'The Association take the view that it would lead to duplication of effort and a wasteful use of resources if the Workers' Educational Association were to be granted providing status as the sister organisations have in England and Wales and in Northern Ireland.'

Even though the Alexander Committee does not go so far as to recommend that the WEA be made a providing body I feel they go pretty far in that direction and I think this is the wrong direction. In my view the Alexander Committee should have recognised the fact that after more than 60 years of existence the WEA in Scotland is largely ineffective and recommended total withdrawal of Government grant aid to the organisation. This would have allowed the other bodies, such as the Education Authorities and Extra-Mural Departments etc to get on with the job of providing an adult education service without competition, duplication and distraction, from the WEA. Organisations like people should be judged by their actions and achievements rather than by pious promises and high hopes.

M T Sweeney

Acknowledgement

The work of the Committee and the presentation of our report owes much to the officers of the Scottish Education Department who have been associated with the Committee. We are indebted to our Assessors, Mr J Kidd, Mr D S Graham, HMI and Mr D McCalman, HMI, who have guided us through the intricacies and complexities of educational administration and policy and have helped us to form our own judgements on which to base recommendations. We are also indebted to the Secretary of the Committee, Mr D R McFarlane and his assistants, Mr J N M Blyth and Mr B McGarry. The life of the Committee has been long and the range of its interests wide, making the work of the Secretary exceptionally onerous. We are grateful to Mr McFarlane for the enthusiasm, patience and efficiency he has contributed.

Appendices

APPENDIX IA

Total Provision*

Year	Student Enrolments	Effective Attendances[1]			
		Male	Female	Total	Total Expressed as % of Post-School Population
1952/53	104,000	Not Available			
1962/63	137,525	Not Available			
1966/67	185,241	41,498	103,781	145,279	3·84
1967/68	184,775	38,024	104,490	142,514	3·80
1968/69	191,789	39,067	109,897	148,964	3·95
1969/70	186,682	36,508	106,399	142,907	3·77
1970/71	205,283	43,536	120,711	164,247	4·36
1971/72	198,886	40,543	109,686	150,229	4·03
1972/73	217,860	45,438	121,528	166,966	4·45

[1]Students who attended two-thirds of the total number of meetings should be regarded as effective attendants.
*Source : Scottish Educational Statistics (HMSO).

APPENDIX IB

Provision by Education Authorities*

Year	Student Enrolments	Effective Attendances[1]		
		Male	Female	Total
1966/67	166,583	35,969	95,379	131,348
1967/68	161,487	31,442	93,749	125,188
1968/69	167,767	31,793	98,742	130,535
1969/70	163,964	30,319	97,039	127,358
1970/71	175,487	34,643	105,404	140,047
1971/72	171,598	33,029	98,464	131,493
1972/73	189,365	37,452	108,738	146,190

[1]Students who attended two-thirds of the total number of meetings should be regarded as effective attendants.
*Source : Scottish Educational Statistics (HMSO).

APPENDIX IC

Provision by Central Institutions*

Year	Student Enrolments	Effective Attendances[1]		
		Male	Female	Total
1966/67	3,467	679	1,888	2,567
1967/68	3,095	615	1,560	2,175
1968/69	2,418	496	1,131	1,627
1969/70	2,448	543	1,095	1,636
1970/71	2,329	451	987	1,438
1971/72	2,510	529	1,003	1,532
1972/73	2,275	503	891	1,394

[1]Students who attended two-thirds of the total number of meetings should be regarded as effective attendants.
*Source : Scottish Educational Statistics (HMSO).

APPENDIX ID

Provision by Extra-Mural Departments *

Year	Student Enrolments	Effective Attendances[1]		
		Male	Female	Total
1966/67	Not Available			
1967/68	18,263	5,125	7,927	13,052
1968/69	19,617	6,391	9,339	15,730
1969/70	18,699	5,086	7,202	12,288
1970/71	24,067	7,791	11,799	19,590
1971/72	20,457	5,721	8,322	14,043
1972/73	21,554	6,147	9,572	15,719

[1]Students who attended two-thirds of the total number of meetings should be regarded as effective attendants.
*Source : Scottish Education Department.

APPENDIX IE

Provision by Workers' Educational Association*

Year	Student Enrolments	Effective Attendances[1]		
		Male	Female	Total
1966/67	Not Available			
1967/68	1,930	576	949	1,525
1968/69	1,987	633	1,006	1,639
1969/70	1,971	560	1,065	1,625
1970/71	3,400	651	2,522	3,173
1971/72	4,321	1,264	1,897	3,161
1972/73	4,666	1,336	2,327	3,663

[1]Students who attended two-thirds of the total number of meetings should be regarded as effective attendants.
*Source: Scottish Education Department.

APPENDIX II

Information Relating to Student Numbers 1968–73

	Year Ending July 1968			Year Ending July 19		
STUDENTS ENROLLING	Male	Female	Total	Male	Female	To
Number	48,312	135,963	184,775	49,912	141,877	191
Number as percentage of total male/female population of 15 years of age and upwards	2·8	6·8	4·9	2·8	7·1	
Number as percentage of total enrolments	26·4	73·6	100·0	26·0	74·0	1
EFFECTIVE STUDENTS						
Number	38,024	104,490	142,514	39,067	109,897	148
Number as percentage of total male/female population of 15 years of age and upwards	2·2	5·2	3·8	2·2	5·5	
Number as percentage of total effective students	26·7	73·3	100·0	26·2	73·8	1
PERCENTAGE OF EFFECTIVE STUDENTS TO NUMBERS ENROLLED	77·8	76·8	77·1	78·3	77·5	

Source : Scottish Education Department
Registrar General, Scotland

	Year Ending July 1970			Year Ending July 1971			Year Ending July 1972			Year Ending July 1973		
	Male	Female	Total	Male	Female	Total	Male	Female	Total	Male	Female	Total
	7,689	138,993	186,682	54,389	150,894	205,283	53,803	145,083	198,886	59,435	158,425	217,860
	2·7	6·9	4·9	3·1	7·5	5·4	3·0	7·2	5·3	3·2	7·4	5·5
	25·5	74·5	100·0	26·5	73·5	100·0	27·1	72·3	100·0	27·3	72·7	100·0
	5,508	106,399	142,907	43,536	120,711	164,247	40,543	109,686	150,229	45,438	121,528	166,966
	2·1	5·3	3·8	2·5	6·0	4·3	2·3	5·5	4·0	2·5	5·6	4·2
	25·5	74·5	100·0	26·5	73·5	100·0	27·0	73·0	100·0	27·2	72·8	100·0
	76·6	76·5	76·6	80·4	80·0	80·0	75·4	75·6	75·5	76·4	76·7	76·6

APPENDIX III

Subjects of Courses followed by Students during 1972/73

| Subject | Education Authorities | | | | Central Institutions | | | |
| | Number Enrolling | | Effective Attendance | | Number Enrolling | | Effective Attendance | |
	Men	Women	Men	Women	Men	Women	Men	Wom
Agriculture and horticulture	193	247	151	200				
Ancient languages and literature	33	31	20	20				
Biological Sciences	134	189	113	166				
Business Studies	164	2,176	123	1,526				
Chemistry								
Cookery	93	7,167	70	5,534				
Economics	72	59	68	53				
English Language and literature	236	356	169	258				
First Aid and Hygiene	550	218	506	174				
General Science	261	265	226	217				
Geography	129	349	107	307				
Handicrafts and Hobbies	15,426	24,580	11,875	19,295	8	18	8	
History	240	459	177	353				
Law								
Mathematics	72	19	52	13				
Modern Languages literature and culture	4,305	6,917	2,789	4,675				
Music	2,262	2,308	1,868	1,873	85	137	72	1
Needlecraft	34	44,409	32	35,982		254		2
Philosophy	27	24	24	10				
Physical Training (including country dancing)	18,561	39,237	14,577	29,141				
Physics	103	132	92	86				
Psychology	45	155	31	103				
Religious Studies	46	78	44	68				
Social Studies	191	610	139	452				
Speech Training and Drama	236	444	196	382	40	122	34	1
Visual Arts	2,377	5,533	1,774	4,088	600	1,011	389	4
Others	2,843	4,770	2,229	3,762				
Totals	48,633	140,732	37,452	108,738	733	1,542	503	8
Total (Men and Women)	189,365		146,190		2,275		1,394	

| University Extra-Mural Committees | | | | Workers' Educational Association | | | | Totals | | | |
| Number Enrolling | | Effective Attendance | | Number Enrolling | | Effective Attendance | | Number Enrolling | | Effective Attendance | |
en	Women	Men	Women	Men	Women	Men	Women	Men	Women	Men	Women
20	11	13	8	23	38	15	26	236	296	179	234
50	30	33	22					83	61	53	42
78	1,452	708	1,118	226	355	187	287	1,338	1,996	1,008	1,571
07	48	76	33	122	57	92	41	393	2,281	291	1,600
16	16	16	16					16	16	16	16
								93	7,167	70	5,534
29	356	475	260					701	415	543	313
95	1,089	306	738	63	67	49	55	794	1,512	524	1,051
								550	218	506	174
30	830	789	627	54	65	49	55	1,345	1,160	1,064	899
15	166	85	122	95	260	80	238	339	775	272	667
20	30	20	30					15,454	24,628	11,903	19,343
11	2,851	1,160	2,137	328	578	277	456	2,079	3,888	1,614	2,946
51	280	121	179	8	3	4	2	159	283	125	181
45	33	33	22					117	52	85	35
87	746	292	460	125	297	89	210	4,917	7,960	3,170	5,345
52	660	246	428	99	253	76	208	2,798	3,358	2,262	2,625
8	33	5	27					42	44,696	37	36,225
90	89	60	49	15	23	9	13	132	136	93	72
20	60	20	60					18,581	39,297	14,597	29,201
								103	132	92	86
30	359	91	246	1	37	—	13	176	551	122	362
55	442	292	312					401	520	336	380
03	1,315	285	976	152	173	103	115	746	2,098	527	1,543
23	32	21	29	86	151	68	135	385	749	319	650
65	1,688	428	1,250	99	199	84	172	3,741	8,431	2,675	5,947
69	569	572	423	204	410	154	301	3,716	5,749	2,955	4,486
69	13,185	6,147	9,572	1,700	2,966	1,336	2,327	59,435	158,425	45,438	121,528
21,554		15,719		4,666		3,663		217,860		166,966	

APPENDIX IV

Information Relating to Certain Popular Courses—1972/73 Education Authorities

Length of Course	Subject	Actual Enrol-ment	%Total Enrol-ment	%Enrolling for Subject		Enrol-ment in listed courses as % of total enrolment
				Male %	Female%	
1 Term	Physical Training	18,749	31·0	30·8	69·2	87·3
	Handicrafts and Hobbies	13,125	21·7	43·2	56·8	
	Needlecraft	11,820	19·6	—	100·0	
	Modern Languages and Culture	3,302	5·5	38·3	61·7	
	Cookery	2,650	4·4	1·4	98·6	
	Visual Arts	2,256	3·7	31·3	68·7	
	Music	861	1·4	50·6	49·4	
2 Terms	Physical Training	32,299	28·9	32·3	67·7	91·5
	Needlecraft	30,083	26·6	0·1	99·9	
	Handicrafts and Hobbies	24,579	21·8	36·6	63·4	
	Modern Languages and Culture	6,566	5·8	38·2	61·8	
	Visual Arts	5,084	4·5	29·9	70·1	
	Cookery	4,388	3·9	1·3	98·7	
3 Terms	Physical Training	6,500	42·2	34·2	65·8	90·5
	Needlecraft	2,472	16·1	—	100·0	
	Handicrafts and Hobbies	2,235	14·5	31·7	68·3	
	Modern Languages and Culture	1,303	8·5	40·3	59·7	
	Music	872	5·7	65·3	34·7	
	Visual Arts	533	3·5	25·1	74·9	
All Courses	Physical Training	57,798	30·5	32·1	67·9	87·6
	Needlecraft	44,443	23·5	0·1	99·9	
	Handicrafts and Hobbies	40,006	21·1	38·6	61·4	
	Modern Languages and Culture	11,222	5·9	38·4	61·6	
	Visual Arts	7,910	4·2	30·1	69·9	
	Music	4,570	2·4	49·5	50·5	

Source : Scottish Education Department.
Scottish Educational Statistics.

University Extra-Mural Departments and Workers' Educational Association

Length of Course	Subject	Actual Enrol- ment	%Total Enrol- ment	%Enrolling for Subject		Enrol- ment in listed courses as % of total enrolment
				Male %	Female%	
1 Term	History	3,122	20·8	38·0	62·0	85·1
	Biological Sciences	2,419	16·1	39·2	60·8	
	Social Studies	1,760	11·7	25·5	74·5	
	Visual Arts	1,210	8·1	28·4	71·6	
	General Science	1,197	8·0	58·1	41·9	
	Economics	677	4·5	63·9	36·1	
	English Language and Literature	630	4·2	38·1	61·9	
2 Terms	History	1,808	18·5	27·9	72·1	73·7
	Visual Arts	1,337	13·7	29·7	70·3	
	English Language and Literature	968	9·9	27·7	72·3	
	Modern Languages and Culture	776	8·0	34·7	65·3	
	Music	761	7·8	32·6	67·4	
	General Science	756	7·7	49·2	50·8	
	Biological Sciences	557	5·7	44·0	56·0	
	Social Studies	215	2·2	35·9	64·1	
3 Terms	Modern Languages and Culture	520	40·6	40·8	59·2	84·1
	History	304	23·7	44·4	55·6	
	English Language and Literature	116	9·0	43·1	56·9	
	Music	71	5·5	29·6	70·4	
	Social Studies	68	5·3	44·1	55·9	
Courses Over One Year	Religious Studies	94	44·3	33·0	67·0	93·3
	Psychology	46	21·7	28·3	71·7	
	History	34	16·0	35·3	64·7	
	Visual Arts	24	11·3	6·7	83·3	
All Courses	History	5,268	20·1	34·9	65·1	75·0
	Biological Sciences	3,011	11·5	40·0	60·0	
	Visual Arts	2,651	10·1	28·8	71·2	
	Social Studies	2,043	7·8	27·2	72·8	
	General Science	1,979	7·5	54·8	45·2	
	English Language and Literature	1,714	6·5	32·6	67·4	
	Modern Languages and Culture	1,655	6·3	37·0	63·0	
	Music	1,364	5·2	33·1	66·9	

Source : Scottish Education Department.
Scottish Educational Statistics.

Central Institutions

Length of Course	Subject	Actual Enrol-ment	% Total Enrol-ment	% Enrolling for Subject		Enrol-ment in listed courses as % of total enrolment
				Male %	Female %	
2 Terms	Visual Arts	1,394	98·2	37·1	62·9	98·2
3 Terms	Music	222	54·7	38·3	61·7	100·0
	Speech Training and Drama	162	39·9	24·7	75·3	
	Visual Arts	22	5·4	9·1	90·9	
Courses over One Year	Needlecraft	254	61·5	—	100·0	100·0
	Visual Arts	159	38·5	35·2	64·8	
All Courses	Visual Arts	1,611	70·8	37·2	62·8	98·9
	Needlecraft	254	11·2	—	100·0	
	Music	222	9·8	38·3	61·7	
	Speech Training and Drama	162	7·1	24·7	75·3	

Source : Scottish Education Department.
Scottish Educational Statistics.

APPENDIX V

Grants Offered in 1972/73 under the Further Education (Scotland) Regulations 1959

(a) Organisations specifically concerned with adult education

Newbattle Abbey College	£47,000
Aberdeen University Extra-Mural Education Committee	4,800
Edinburgh University Extra-Mural Education Committee	6,300
Glasgow University Extra-Mural Education Committee	8,100
Dundee University Extra-Mural Education Committee	2,900
Workers' Educational Association :	
North of Scotland District	7,050
South-East Scotland District	7,050
West of Scotland District	9,500
Scottish Council	530
Scottish Institute of Adult Education	3,300

(b) Other organisations who have an interest in adult education

An Comunn Gaidhealach	12,000
Board for Information on Youth and Community Service	9,400
Community Service Volunteers	3,200
Conservation Corps	2,625
Duke of Edinburgh's Award Scheme	3,000
Endeavour Training	1,000
Enterprise Youth	10,500
Moray Sea School (Outward Bound)	4,450
Scottish Amateur Music Association	950
Scottish Association of Young Farmers' Clubs	4,500
Scottish Community Drama Association	10,000
Scottish Council of Social Service	500
Scottish Field Studies Association	1,000
Scottish Joint YMCA/YWCA Committee	2,150
Scottish National Council of YMCAs	7,500
Scottish Pipe Band Association	1,750
Scottish Women's Rural Institutes	700
Toc H : Loch Eil Centre	3,950
West Highland School of Adventure	1,600
YWCA of Great Britain	6,600
YWCA of Scotland	1,250

APPENDIX VI

Staffing of Organisations Specifically Concerned with Adult Education who received Grant during 1972/73 under the Further Education (Scotland) Regulations 1959

Organisation	Teachers/Lecturers		Admin Staff		Remarks
	Full-time	Part-time	Full-time	Part-time	
Newbattle Abbey College	3	6	1*	—	*Bursar
WEA					
North of Scotland District	1	—	1	—	
South-East Scotland	1	—	1	—	
West of Scotland	3	—	1	—	
Scottish Council	—	—	—	—	
University EMC					
Aberdeen	4	192	2*	—	
Dundee	—	307	2*	1	
Edinburgh	2	203	4*	—	
Glasgow	16	669	5	1	
St Andrews	—	168	1*	2	*Admin and Teaching combined
Scottish Institute of Adult Education	—	—	1	—	Secretary
TOTALS	30	1,545	19	4	

APPENDIX VII

NEWBATTLE ABBEY COLLEGE
Grants in Respect of Revenue Expenditure

(a)

Year	From Scottish Education Department	From Education Authorities	From Other Sources including fees etc
	£	£	£
1967/68	23,000	2,878	25,621
1968/69	26,250	3,051	28,710
1969/70	23,000	2,661	28,050
1970/71	41,000	2,869	29,623
1971/72	37,560	2,937	27,417
1972/73	47,000	2,786	30,106

In addition capital grant of £240,000 was incurred during 1964 and 1973 towards the cost of new residential accommodation and alterations to the existing premises. £168,000 of the total grant was provided by the Scottish Education Department, and the remainder by education authorities, other organisations and individuals.

Number and Areas of Origin of Students Attending Sessional Course

(b)

Year	Scotland	Elsewhere in United Kingdom	Overseas	Total
1967/68	26	41	—	67
1968/69	18	44	3	65
1969/70	23	42	2	67
1970/71	32	36	1	69
1971/72	25	36	3	64
1972/73	18	48	2	68

Short Courses

(c)

Year	Number of Courses Provided	Total Enrolments
1967/68	12	477
1968/69	14	616
1969/70	12	562
1970/71	12	560
1971/72	10	458
1972/73	11	595

APPENDIX VIII

Diploma Course in Adult Education
Provision by the Universities of Edinburgh and Glasgow during Session 1973–74

(Course extends over two academic years (part-time) or one academic year (full-time))

Edinburgh

Full-time Students—15 (all graduates)
Part-time Students—Nil
Areas of origin of students—Scotland 5, England 4, Ireland 1, Overseas 5

Of the 10 UK students, most were young graduates with no full-time work behind them but who intended to go into adult education full-time either as teachers or as administrators. Two were mature students with little adult education background or teaching experience but who had a desire to work in adult education. It is generally accepted that the UK students will have no difficulty in finding employment in adult education in England but little chance of them finding a post in adult education in Scotland.

Glasgow

Full-time Students—Nil
Part-time Students—22
Graduates   —16
Qualified Teachers—17
Areas of origin of students—Scotland 17, England 4, Overseas 1

On completion of the course 18 of the students proposed to work, or continue to work in adult education, either full-time or part-time. 17 of them were already employed full-time in adult education and one part-time. The remaining 4 were unlikely to change their present employment. Their occupations were:

Educational Psychologist   2
Government Training Centre Manager   1
General Secretary, United Nations Association 1

APPENDIX IX

**Youth and Community Service
Education Authority Provision**

Year	Membership of Local Units, Club, Centres, etc		Number of Youth Service Organisers, Leaders and Specialist Instructors Employed by Education Authorities		Value of assistance provided by Education Authorities to Adult and Youth Clubs
	Number of Units	Membership			
	1	2	3	4	5
			Total	Full-time (included in 3)	£
1967/68	751	78,699	3,984	104	506,937
1968/69	817	81,510	4,161	143	560,937
1969/70	777	80,630	4,668	162	685,971
1970/71	813	81,916	5,067	196	758,539
1971/72	951	118,487	7,177	287	930,195
1972/73	986	131,964	7,135	328	837,286

APPENDIX X

Central Institutions in Receipt of Grant under the Further Education (Scotland) Regulations 1959

Robert Gordon's Institute of Technology, Aberdeen
Dundee Institute of Art and Technology
Leith Nautical College, Edinburgh
Edinburgh College of Art
Edinburgh College of Domestic Science
Glasgow School of Art
Royal Scottish Academy of Music and Drama, Glasgow
Glasgow and West of Scotland College of Domestic Science
Paisley College of Technology
Scottish College of Textiles, Galashiels, Selkirkshire

APPENDIX XI

University Extra-Mural Committee Areas

Aberdeen University

Member Education Authorities: Aberdeen City, Aberdeen County, Banff, Caithness, Inverness, Kincardine, Moray and Nairn, Orkney, Ross and Cromarty, Sutherland, Zetland.

Dundee University

Member Education Authorities: Angus, Clackmannan, Dundee, Perth and Kinross.

Edinburgh University

Member Education Authorities: Berwick, East Lothian, Edinburgh, Midlothian, Peebles, Roxburgh, Selkirk, West Lothian.

Glasgow University

Member Education Authorities: Argyll, Ayr, Bute, Dunbarton, Dumfries, Glasgow, Kirkcudbright, Lanark, Renfrew, Stirling, Wigtown.

Note: Fife Education Authority operates independently and work in the area is carried out by its own tutor-organisers, usually in collaboration with the Extra-Mural Department in St Andrews.

APPENDIX XII

Report on a Survey Carried out by the Committee

It has already been pointed out that the statistics relating to voluntary leisure time courses for adults collected annually by the Scottish Education Department were inadequate for the Committee's purposes. To supplement them a questionnaire was sent to all education authorities requesting information for 1971/72 (ie the latest complete year at the time when the questionnaire was circulated) and for 1966/67 in order to try to assess changes over the five-year period.

Presentation of Results

The questionnaires were sent to all 35 education authorities. Three authorities (representing some 4 per cent of the population aged 15 or over in June 1972) did not reply. The remaining 32 co-operated but in some cases the information returned was incomplete and much of the information given was based on estimates. This was not unexpected since details of non-vocational adult education are not normally classified as a separate category in the statistical records maintained by both central and local government. In particular, the information provided about 1966/67 was so limited that no worthwhile comparison with 1971/72 could be made. The main statistical summaries derived from the replies are detailed in the following tables. Where tables give information by regions these correspond to Planning Regions included in the Annual Report of the Registrar General Scotland 1972. Composition of the regions is as follows:

Region	Education Authority Areas
Glasgow	Glasgow City; Lanark; Renfrew; Bute; Dunbarton; Ayr.
Falkirk/Stirling	Clackmannan; Stirling.
Edinburgh	Edinburgh City; The Lothians; Fife.
Tayside	Dundee City; Angus; Perth and Kinross.
Borders	Berwick; Peebles; Roxburgh; Selkirk.
South West	Wigtown; Kirkcudbright; Dumfries.
North East	Aberdeen City; Aberdeen; Kincardine; Banff; Moray and Nairn.
Highlands	Argyll; Caithness; Inverness; Orkney; Ross and Cromarty; Sutherland; Zetland.

Organisation, Staffing and Staff Courses

Of the 32 authorities who replied 2 indicated that no committee or sub-committee had a specific responsibility for adult education: in 27 cases it was the responsibility of a sub-committee with further education generally; and in 3 cases responsibility lay with a schools sub-committee. Most of the sub-committees mentioned also had responsibility for youth and community services libraries and youth employment. The administrative staff responsible for adult education were usually headed by a depute or assistant director; there was some variation in the proportion of their time spent on adult education but a figure of 10 per cent was not uncommon. Details of both administrative and non-administrative staff in post in 1971/72 are summarised in Table 1. Of the courses provided by education authorities specifically for adult education staff in 1971/72, 5 were for adult education principals and 24 for adult education teachers. In addition 13 full-time staff attended other courses in adult education, all of which were of less than one month's duration.

Courses Provided for Special Groups

A summary of the enrolments in 1971/72 of courses provided for special groups is given in Table 2. Twelve of the responding authorities submitted a nil return for all categories of provision. Community centres account for 63 per cent of the total provision, 80 per cent of it being in Glasgow, Dundee or Lanark. The 'Other' category includes such provision as field

115

study, parents' associations, enjoying retirement, personnel in pre-school playgroups and YMCA. The numbers in the Table relate only to classes for which financial assistance was given by the education authority; thus, for example, the numbers involved in Townswomen's Guild's and SWRI activities greatly exceed those given here.

Building Projects

Of the 32 education authorities who replied to the questionnaire 25 gave details of building projects, including contributions to capital expenditure for projects undertaken by other bodies (abbreviated to 'other projects' in Table 3), in the period 1966–67 to 1971–72. The replies are summarised in Table 3.

Of the 207 projects costing £5 million, 157 (76 per cent of the projects and 60 per cent of the total expenditure) related to community centres and village halls. In relation to the 50 projects to provide premises other than community centres and village halls, 38 of these were to provide wings or suites of rooms for adult education in schools.

Expenditure and Income

From the comments appended to the completed questionnaires, it was clear that most education authorities had difficulty in providing details of the expenditure and income for non-vocational adult education. Many of the figures provided were estimated apportionments. Details for 1971/72 were provided by authorities representing 73 per cent of the population aged 15 and over and a regional breakdown has been provided (Table 4) for consistency with the other data collected; any comparisons drawn from this Table would be very misleading. Transfer payments between education authorities are included under 'other income'.

The estimated net expenditure on adult education represents about 0·9 per cent of the total net expenditure by education authorities on all services.

TABLE 1
Education Authorities' Adult Education Staff in Post: 1971/72

OTHER THAN ADMINISTRATION STAFF	Glasgow	Falkirk/ Stirling	Edinburgh	Tayside	Borders	South West	North East	Highlands	TOTAL
EA organisers or advisers wholly or mainly employed in adult education									
Number	4	—	—	—	—	—	—	—	4
Full-time equivalent	1	—	—	—	—	—	—	—	1
Full-time adult education principals	5	—	9	—	1	—	3	—	18
Principals whose full-time appointment is shared between adult education and other duties									
Number	23	1	1	1	6	2	—	—	34
Full-time equivalent	9	—	—	—	1	—	—	—	10
Part-time adult education principals	298	47	135	23	23	59	56	123	764
Full-time adult education teachers	6	—	—	—	—	—	—	—	6
Part-time adult education teachers	3,494	979	2,510	454	178	256	1,241	555	9,667
Full-time community centre wardens etc	45	1	7	4	2	—	23	1	83
ADMINISTRATIVE STAFF									
Administrative officers responsible to director of education for adult education	31	2	12	4	3	5	10	7	74
Possible number of replies	6	2	5	3	4	3	5	7	35
Actual number of replies	6	2	4	3	3	3	5	6	32

TABLE 2
Enrolments on all Courses Provided by Education Authorities for Special Groups in 1971–72

	Community Centres	Handicapped	Hospital Patients	Semi-Literate Adults	Industrial Groups	Old People	Preparation for Retirement	Prisons, Borstals and Detention Centres	Townswomen's Guilds	SWRI	Other	TOTAL
GLASGOW	9,882	394	546	147	20	237	405	300	100	50	200	12,281
FALKIRK/STIRLING	244	—	—	20	—	400	8	1,126	—	—	—	1,798
EDINBURGH	298	309	83	11	351	1,036	115	140	71	—	666	3,080
TAYSIDE	3,312	199	40	—	—	822	—	220	—	576	60	5,229
BORDERS	20	17	—	—	—	12	—	110	20	—	—	179
SOUTH WEST	—	—	—	—	—	—	—	—	—	—	—	—
NORTH EAST	1,785	97	—	—	10	—	—	76	—	—	189	2,158
HIGHLANDS	—	32	—	—	—	—	—	—	—	—	—	32
TOTAL SCOTLAND	15,542	1,048	669	178	381	2,507	528	1,972	191	626	1,115	24,757
Number of respondents making provisions	13	10	4	4	3	8	7	9	4	2	4	

TABLE 3
Building Projects Started 1966–67 to 1971–72 Reported by Education Authorities

	GLASGOW		FALKIRK/ STIRLING		EDINBUR	
	Projects (No)	Net Cost (£'000)	Projects (No)	Net Cost (£'000)	Projects (No)	(£'C
COMMUNITY CENTRES AND VILLAGE HALLS: Projects started by the EA:						
Community Centres	13	912·9	6	329·1	8	4
Village Halls	—	—	—	—	2	
Wings or suites of rooms	2	62·0	—	—	2	
TOTAL	15	974·9	6	329·1	12	6
Other Projects	1	0·1	—	—	25	1
TOTAL	16	975·0	6	329·1	37	7
PREMISES OTHER THAN COMMUNITY CENTRES AND VILLAGE HALLS Projects started by the EA:						
Premises built specifically for Adult Education	—	—	—	—	—	
Premises converted for Adult Education	1	0·5	—	—	—	
Wings or suites of rooms provided for Adult Education in:						
Schools	22	750·0	4	98·0	2	N/
FE establishments	—	—	—	—	4	1
TOTAL	23	750·5	4	98·0	6	1
Other Projects	—	—	—	—	1	6
TOTAL	23	750·5	4	98·0	7	7
No of authorities starting projects	5		2		4	
No of authorities returning questionnaires	6		2		4	
Total number of authorities	6		2		5	

120

	TAYSIDE		BORDERS		SOUTH WEST		NORTH EAST		HIGHLANDS		TOTAL	
Projects (No)	Projects (No)	Net Cost (£'000)	Projects (No)	Net Cost (£'000)	Projects (No)	Net Cost (£'000)	Projects (No)	Net Cost (£'000)	Projects (No)	Net Cost (£'000)	Projects (No)	Net Cost (£'000)
3		350·0	1	N/avail	—	—	12	498·0	1	15·0	44	2569·0
—		—	—	—	—	—	—	—	—	—	2	90·0
2		16·0	—	—	—	—	8	16·1	2	30·0	16	198·1
5		366·0	1	N/avail	—	—	20	514·1	3	45·0	62	2857·1
3		0·9	1	1·8	—	—	44	42·2	21	12·8	95	175·1
8		366·9	2	1·8	—	—	64	556·3	24	57·8	157	3032·2
1		150·0	—	—	—	—	—	—	—	—	1	150·0
—		—	—	—	—	—	1	21·4	—	—	2	21·9
6		90·6	—	—	—	—	3	13·0	1	54·0	38	1005·6
—		—	—	—	—	—	—	—	—	—	4	125·7
7		240·6	—	—	—	—	4	34·4	1	54·0	45	1303·2
—		—	—	—	—	—	2	1·4	2	0·8	5	662·2
7		240·6	—	—	—	—	6	35·8	3	54·8	50	1965·4
3			2		0		5		4		25	
3			3		3		5		6		32	
3			4		3		5		7		35	

TABLE 4
Expenditure and Income on Adult Education by Education Authorities: 1971/72

Region	Glasgow	Falkirk/Stirling	Edinburgh	Tayside	Borders	South West	North East	Highlands
Expenditure:								
Salaries and Wages								
Head Office Staff:								
Administrative and Clerical	7,160	400	*108,620	13,430	*6,548	750	42	7,720
Inspectors and Organisers	4,423	350	*Incl. above	4,740	*Incl. above	622	*57,792	16,319
Teachers:								
Full- and Part-Time	377,302	14,321	*Incl. above	105,472	*Incl. above	18,128	*Incl. above	30,319
Clerical Assistants, Cleaners, Caretakers and Others	215,624	9,234	31,246	60,956	200	1,942	9,702	6,313
Repairs, Maintenance, Fuel, Light, Cleaning Materials, Water	117,957	942	19,000	65,295	4,721	4,550	18,300	5,467
Furniture, Fittings, Rent, Rates, Equipment, Tools, Materials	109,251	4,032	80,201	32,234	1,657	391	4,001	7,071
Telephones, Printing, Stationery, Postage, Advertising	13,999	450	1,595	2,544	158	809	315	610
Grants to Responsible and other Bodies	11,111	4,907	—	7,769	1,039	1,010	7,215	7,487
Travelling and Subsistence	6,213	—	900	6,338	850	1,019	7,605	5,848
Awards to Students	9,350	24,653	—	15	—	—	—	7,931
Loan Charges	24,000	—	—	49,000	—	—	—	—
Other Expenditure	31,973	5,040	600	5,454	458	4,793	8	134
Total Expenditure	928,363	64,329	242,162	353,247	15,631	34,014	104,980	95,097

TABLE 4 (contd)

Region	Glasgow	Falkirk/Stirling	Edinburgh	Tayside	Borders	South West	North East	Highlands
Income								
Tuition Fees	73,499	2,600	29,743	27,932	1,926	9,826	17,227	5,661
Other Income	25,265	6,695	7,151	34,912	543	614	1,742	3,920
Total Income	98,764	9,295	36,894	62,844	2,469	10,440	18,969	9,581
Net Expenditure								
On Adult Education	829,599	55,034	205,268	290,403	13,162	23,574	86,011	85,516
By EAs on all Services	105,536,320	1,949,535	21,281,226	18,501,760	2,030,473	5,206,763	11,114,518	10,823,313
Possible Number of Returns	6	2	5	3	4	3	5	7
Actual Number of Returns	5	1	2	3	2	2	3	6

APPENDIX XIII

Report on Case Studies Carried out on Behalf of the Committee

The aim of conducting these case studies was to try and construct a profile of students who attend adult education classes so as to aid the formulation of future adult education policy.

A strict statistical comparison of data derived from the 4 case studies is not possible; there was considerable variation in all the studies, and the numbers quoted below are average assessments only. This in part reflects the different types of area surveyed (urban, rural, and urban/rural). Furthermore only a single representative was drawn from each area. Another point to note is the poor rate of return particularly for education authority classes:

Argyll	—	450 returns from 560 distributed
Dundee	—	292 returns from 486 distributed
Fife	—	366 returns from 500 distributed
St Andrews	—	67 returns from 100 distributed

These figures give a response rate of some 70 per cent.

The Existing Population

In all areas the majority of the students were women, the mean percentage being 64 (in Fife it was as high as 75). The mean percentage of married students was 63 and some 58 per cent had no children of 16 or under in their care. A contributory factor in the latter case is certainly age where again there was considerable variation between the selected areas. The under 25 age group was poorly represented (15 per cent on average), and 27 per cent of students were over age 55. There was a reasonably uniform spread of ages between 25 and 55.

Figures for the period of students' domicile tend to suggest that adult education students are not highly 'mobile'. This is consistent with the small numbers of students in the younger age range, which is the most 'mobile' in respect of house and/or employment. Approximately 65 per cent of students involved in the questionnaire had lived in the areas surveyed for more than 5 years.

With respect to background of full-time education, there was considerable variation between areas. The proportion of students who had finished their full-time education at age 15 or under varied from 15 (Argyll EMC) to 47 (Fife); the mean percentage for those finishing at age 16 or less varied from 27 (Argyll FE) to 63 (Fife) with a mean of 44. The implication was therefore that a sizeable proportion of adult education students possessed some further or higher educational qualifications and this was to some extent confirmed by the case study results which showed that more than 20 per cent of the students had a university degree or its equivalent.

Analysis of the answers to the question which asked for a specification of students' regular work showed between 83 and 88 per cent of students in the top 3 classes of the Registrar General's 6 point socio-economic scale, except for Argyll EA which assumed a value of 55 per cent. This relatively high socio-economic status of the respondents was reflected in low figures for trade union membership (mean of 8 per cent) and higher figures for membership of a professional association (mean of 19 per cent including a very low figure for Argyll of 6 per cent).

Analysis of the returns pointed to the following factors being the main motives for students attending classes: special interest in a subject, general cultural/educational interest, learning/making something for home life, using leisure time more positively and constructively.

Changes over Time and Recruitment

The figures for those attending an adult education class for the first time were small; all areas except Argyll FE showed that at least 55 per cent of the students had previously attended a class of this type (in Argyll the figure was 27 per cent), indicating a marked degree of continuity of student participation.

Enquiry as to how those attending classes first learned about the provision produced the following information:

a. attendance at a previous class (22 per cent);
b. recommendation by a friend (20 per cent);
c. newspaper advertisement (20 per cent);
d. brochure/circular from the organisers (12 per cent);
e. personal enquiry (8 per cent).

The figures showed some variation from area to area, but the other sources of information such as notices, posters etc at places of work, public libraries etc were consistently very low.

Students' Opinions of Courses

Overall, some 67 per cent thought the course they were attending was of the correct length, 19 per cent thought that the time allowed was inadequate and a negligible percentage believed their course to be too long.

General satisfaction was recorded with other factors relating to the course. For example, 32 per cent stated that the course had turned out better than expected and 51 per cent affirmed that it was as good as they had hoped; only a small percentage found fault. Similar satisfaction was indicated by the very low mean value of 2 per cent of students finding the courses poor value for expenditure.

In reply to the questions regarding work done in class, 78 per cent found that the course was 'just right' in terms of difficulty. The fact that few people will ever admit to a course being too difficult, more especially in regard to a 'recreational' area of learning, is reflected in the very small figure of 2 per cent who found their course too difficult. Some 5 per cent found their course too easy.

An analysis of students' opinions on the standard of teaching showed that 74 per cent found it 'good' and 15 per cent thought it 'average'; a very small percentage indicated dissatisfaction.

Only 7 per cent of students found the accommodation unsuitable. However, just under 15 per cent held the view that the equipment or material provided was less than adequate. Clearly even with wholly adequate data, conclusions in an area such as this must be made with great care since every subject may differ in its teaching method and reliance on teaching aids.

The final point relates to the availability of courses within areas. Except for Argyll (12 per cent) a high percentage of students believed that there was a wide choice of courses within their area. Fife had a figure of 56, Dundee 69 and St Andrews 73. Taking into account the large number of respondents who believed the choice available to be average, it is reasonable to suppose that dissatisfaction with the choice of classes which existed was minimal with the exception of 'rural' Argyll. This is not a cause for great surprise since people would probably only attend those classes which interested them and would not consider the omission of a subject outwith their field of interest as a defect in the provision.

Summary and Conclusion

The following list enumerates the main pointers emerging from the case studies:

i. women form a high proportion of the students;
ii. there are few students aged below 25 but about a quarter are over 55;
iii. a large proportion of the students are married;
iv. adult education students tend not to be 'mobile';
v. there is a marked degree of continuity of student participation, suggesting satisfaction to a considerable extent with the way classes are run.

vi.   there is an indication of a sizeable proportion, about a quarter on average, of students with further or higher educational qualifications;

vii. students as a whole have relatively high socio-economic status;

viii. the main motivating factors appear to be:
    a. special interest in a subject
    b. general cultural/educational interest
    c. a wish to learn/make something useful for home life
    d. a wish to use leisure time more positively
    e. a wish for relaxation.

In conclusion we should like to emphasise that all the data analysed and presented here related to students already committed to adult education courses. We have sought to find out something about adult education students and how they see the system from within. The case studies were not meant to explore the characteristics of the population who, although eligible to attend adult education classes, were not doing so or to find out why they did not attend, what would interest them and what would motivate them sufficiently to make them attend.

APPENDIX XIV

Report on a Survey carried out by the Committee on Training for Trade Unionists and Shop Stewards

The main agency stimulating interest in and demand for education for trade unionists is the Trades Union Congress Education Service, provided under the aegis of the Trades Union Congress, and served in Scotland by one full-time official. This service provides in-plant and week-end courses and, in conjunction with various further education colleges, supports other educational work among trade unionists. The Workers' Educational Association also has a close involvement in such work, operating mainly as an agent of the TUCES but also providing some evening classes specially designed to interest and attract trade unionists.

In addition some Industrial Training Boards have encouraged shop-steward training in Scotland, either by themselves organising and providing courses or by making a financial contribution to such courses (or elements in courses) provided by particular firms. Since 1973 the Industrial Society has also made a small contribution to total provision in this area, by organising short courses and seminars for shop stewards. A number of unions organise their own week and week-end residential courses. The Scottish Trades Union Congress provides a small but effective educational programme for the members of affiliated unions. In addition to an annual summer school of one week's duration and a number of week-end courses for young trade unionists and women trade unionists, day and week-end schools are organised on subjects of current interest and importance to trade unionists. The extra-mural departments of the Scottish universities have not been particularly active in this field.

This Appendix sets out the activities of the TUCES and of the colleges, which together provide most of the training facilities available to shop stewards.

Trades Union Congress Education Service

Over nine years to 1974 the Service has provided 106 in-plant day release courses (mostly of five days duration) for shop stewards employed by some 45 companies. In addition the Service has been involved in the provision of day-release courses in commercial and technical colleges. This is a type of provision which is developing and the number of participating colleges increasing. It also provides residential week-end schools, full-day schools and evening classes and operating from Tillicoultry, provides correspondence courses for students in all parts of the United Kingdom.

126

Technical Colleges and Colleges of Commerce

In February 1973 a questionnaire was sent to all colleges in Scotland thought to be offering courses for shop stewards. Although this has been a largely neglected area of education in Scotland the returns indicated a growth in provision over a two-year period.

Year	1971/72	1972/73
Number of colleges	4	8
Total number of courses	15	29
Total number of students	274	482

Thirteen colleges intimated that they planned to conduct courses in shop steward training in 1973/74. Those colleges who provided returns to the questionnaire are listed below along with those who planned to offer such courses during 1973/74.

1971/72	Glasgow College of Building and Printing
	Glenrothes and Buckhaven Technical College
	Kirkcaldy Technical College
	Paisley College of Technology
1972/73	Central College of Commerce, Glasgow
	Dumfries Technical College
	Edinburgh College of Commerce
	Glasgow College of Building and Printing
	Glenrothes and Buckhaven Technical College
	James Watt College, Greenock
	Kirkcaldy Technical College
	Paisley College of Technology
1973/74	*Aberdeen Technical College
	*Bell College of Technology, Hamilton
	*Central College of Commerce, Glasgow
	*Coatbridge Technical College
	Dumfries Technical College
	*Dundee College of Commerce
	*Edinburgh College of Commerce
	Falkirk Technical College
	Glasgow College of Building and Printing
	Glenrothes and Buckhaven Technical College
	*James Watt College, Greenock
	*Kirkcaldy Technical College
	Paisley College of Technology

*Courses to be mounted in co-operation with the TUC (Scotland) Education Service.

A more detailed examination of the returns provided the following information:

1971/72

Eight courses were attended on a block release basis (one of which was wholly residential lasting five days) and 7 on a part-time release basis.

Nine courses were planned by the colleges themselves; 5 jointly by the colleges, local trade unions and employers; and 1 by a college and a local trade union.

Eight courses were staffed jointly by full-time college staff, part-time college staff and trade union officials; 6 staffed jointly by full-time college staff and trade union officials; and 1 staffed by full-time college staff only.

The course fee was paid in 9 instances by employers; twice by employers and trades unions; twice by employers and Industrial Training Boards; once by an Industrial Training Board alone; and once by a trade union.

1972/73

Sixteen courses were attended on a block release basis; 7 on evenings only; 5 on a part-time day release basis; and 1 on a full-time basis (partly residential).

Nine courses were planned by the employers; 8 planned jointly by the colleges concerned, employers and local trades unions; 4 planned by the colleges themselves; 3 planned jointly by the colleges and Industrial Training Boards; 2 planned by local trades unions; 2 planned jointly by the colleges, local trades unions and Industrial Training Boards; and 1 by an employer and a local trade union.

Twelve courses were staffed jointly by full-time college staff, trade union officials and others including industrialists and employers; 6 staffed jointly by full-time college staff, part-time college staff and others; 4 staffed jointly by full-time college staff and trade union officials; 3 staffed jointly by full-time college staff, part-time college staff and trade union officials; 2 staffed jointly by full-time college staff, part-time college staff, trade union officials and others including civil servants and employers; 1 by full-time college staff and civil servants; and 1 by full-time college staff only.

The course fee was paid in 16 instances by the employers; in 7 instances by the employers and the trades unions; in 3 instances by the trades unions; twice by Industrial Training Boards; and once by the employer, the trade union and the Industrial Training Board.

Courses and Schools Arranged by TUC (Scotland) Education Service

	Weekend Schools Number Attendances	Day Schools Number Attendances	Day Release Courses Number Attendances	Evening Classes Number Attendances
Sept 1968 Aug 1969	38....891	26....782	18....297	13....206
Sept 1969 Aug 1970	36....780	18....559	9....140	8....113
Sept 1970 Aug 1971	31....761	20....684	2.... 37	8....124
Sept 1971 Aug 1972	33....760	31....942	17....227	9....152
Sept 1972 Aug 1973	32....605	14....422	13....252	6....108
Sept 1973 Aug 1974	29....432	22....500	21....350	5.... 77

APPENDIX XV

SCOTTISH CERTIFICATE OF EDUCATION EXAMINATION BOARD CANDIDATES OTHER THAN SCHOOL CANDIDATES

Number of Candidates

	'O' Grade Only	At Least One Higher
1965	11,424	4,714
1966	13,641	6,372
1967	14,931	7,911
1968	15,658	10,139
1969	16,241	12,237
1970	15,192	13,433
1971	14,188	13,981
1972	12,344	14,190
1973	11,248	12,747

Subject Presentation

	'O' Grade	'H' Grade
1965	23,432	6,779
1966	26,886	9,116
1967	29,232	11,159
1968	30,341	14,344
1969	31,595	17,322
1970	29,755	19,073
1971	28,625	20,551
1972	25,718	21,182
1973	22,971	19,213

Source: Scottish Certificate of Education Examination Board.

APPENDIX XVI

THE OPEN UNIVERSITY IN SCOTLAND

Number of Applications Received and the Number who Subsequently Accepted Places Offered

Year Commencing January	Total Applicants	Total Students
1971	3,163	2,136
1972	2,910	1,773
1973	2,957	1,528
1974	3,078	1,273

Note: (1) The decrease in the number of places taken up is due partly to a reduction of funds available and partly because of the growing number of continuing students each year.
(2) At October 1973 there were 2,967 under-graduate students and 188 post-experience students in Scotland.

APPENDIX XVII

KJWA :ag   Thursday 28 March 1974

The Rt Hon William Ross, PC MP
HM Secretary of State for Scotland
St Andrew's House
EDINBURGH EH1

Dear Mr Ross

The Committee on Adult Education in Scotland of which I am Chairman, have received evidence from both individuals and organisations about the role and potential of television and radio in adult education. In particular, arguments have been put to us on the question whether there is need for a fourth television channel and, if so, whether it should be devoted solely to educational programmes. Against the possibility that a Government decision may be taken on the issue before our report is completed my Committee have agreed that I should convey to you an outline of their views on the matter.

I should perhaps explain that although as a Committee we are concerned with the non-vocational education of adults in their leisure time, our membership includes persons who in various ways are involved in every other sector of the educational field. We assume, however, that the views of these various sectors have been or will be advanced by others. Our concern is simply to express an adult education view. We consider that the present and prospective needs of adult education are such as to present a compelling case for an additional television channel. We would not support any suggestion that such a channel should be devoted exclusively to educational programmes, however.

The arguments in favour of an additional channel include the following :

(a)   There is clear evidence of a growing demand by adults for educational programmes of high quality and further evidence that this demand is likely to show steady increase in future.

(b)   The ability of television to make a significant contribution towards meeting this demand is already established.

(c)   Television is a cost-effective method of meeting the needs of large numbers of students and potential students who find it difficult or impossible, because of the nature of their employment, the isolation of their homes or physical or other handicap, to attend classes organised on conventional lines.

(d)   Such educational programmes as are provided on the three existing channels are steadily being relegated to very late and other off-peak times which are suitable for only a limited proportion of those who wish to see them and which provide no opportunity for capturing the interest of those not already committed.

(e)   In addition to educational programmes in general being squeezed out of good viewing times by entertainment programmes the competing and growing needs of the various sectors of education exert further pressures which, unless more television time over all can be provided, must inevitably exacerbate present difficulties.

In our view there are particular kinds of adult educational programmes which are especially appropriate to television, eg education about the environment, including conservation, design education and the visual arts generally; and experience has shown that while language teaching may be less dependent on the visual medium it can be made substantially more effective and popular by television presentation. There is also a need for a greater frequency and regularity of programmes if the benefits of more intensive teaching are to be secured. However, development along these lines is not possible without an increase in the number of programme hours allocated to adult education and particularly in the number of hours at peak and near-peak viewing times. The only solution appears to us to be to provide an additional channel and thus secure an increase in the total number of viewing hours.

As I have already indicated we do not think that an additional channel should be devoted exclusively to educational programmes. We recognise that there are opposing opinions on this question but, having examined the arguments on both sides, we are convinced that the advantages to be gained from a channel devoted to educational programmes would be outweighed by the disadvantages. For example, we assume that such a channel, if created, would be expected to absorb all the educational programmes at present distributed among the existing channels and that the latter would thereafter concentrate on news, current affairs, general entertainment and indeed all the programmes which attract the bulk of the viewing public. If this is so we are convinced that the inevitable consequence would be to create a situation in which only those with a positive commitment to study would tune in to the educational channel. In our view it is highly desirable that the existing diversity of provision should be maintained on all channels, that any increase in distributing capacity provided by a fourth channel should be allocated with the growing needs of adult education in mind and that there should be clear and precise stipulations as to programme balance and the allocation of good viewing times. We are particularly concerned that adult educational programmes should be given more time in the evenings and at weekends when the average adult has leisure time available, at times which would enable classes and other activities to be based on them and for them to be interspersed with general entertainment programmes in order that viewers might carry over from a news or entertainment programme to an educational programme and as a result develop an interest in the educational subject.

We have also considered the situation with regard to the administration of educational broadcasting generally in the event of an increase in the amount of television time allocated to it. The claims, no doubt often conflicting, of the various sectors of education, including school, post school vocational and non-vocational, Open University and special needs, suggest to us the desirability of setting up two new national bodies, one an executive body, the other a 'watchdog' body and both appointed by Government. The former, which might be called the Educational Broadcasting Authority, should have a small membership which is not predominantly educational in composition in order to avoid any suggestion of vested interests which might operate to the advantage of one sector of education at the expense of others. It should have responsibility for securing the most effective use of the broadcasting time available to it on both television and radio. It should have an annual budget provided by Government and have the power to buy programme time or be given an annual allocation of programme time on all channels, including prime hours. It should have power to determine educational programme policy, including the allocation of programme times among the various educational interests and power to produce its own programmes or to sub-contract production on lines similar to those already adopted for the Open University. In addition it should be required to have particular regard to the varying needs of the different regions of the country. In suggesting this we have in mind the need to safeguard the position of Scotland where now, perhaps more than ever before, there are great and growing difficulties of isolation on the one hand and rapid development on the other which are quite unique in the United Kingdom and require special treatment of a kind to which the broadcasting media are capable of making an important contribution.

As regards the watchdog body, we are aware that there are already in existence various such bodies representing particular aspects or areas of education. We understand that these bodies operate largely independently of each other and we think it better that they should be replaced by a single body, which should have within its membership representatives of the Scottish Education Department and the Department of Education and Science, and of the various sectors of education including the development councils (as recommended in the Russell Report on Adult Education in England and Wales and those we shall recommend for Scotland). The task to be given to this body should be to maintain a general oversight over the work of the Educational Broadcasting Authority, to give assistance and advice on any matter relating to educational broadcasting at the request of the EBA and to submit an annual report to Government on the work of the EBA, including any suggestions or recommendations for the improvement of the service generally.

We also recommend that any additional television channel should be based on the BBC rather than the independent companies, partly because of the former's recognised superiority in the field but also because this would provide greater scope for cross-linking with the other two BBC channels. In addition, however, we feel that to have two commercial channels, both striving to reach mass audiences in order to secure the advertising revenue necessary for their survival, could lead to an undesirable lowering in programme standards; and that the BBC might be forced into a corresponding lowering of standards simply in order to maintain its audience levels.

We are at present looking into the question of the probable costs of implementing these proposals and we hope to include a reference to this in our report.

Perhaps I may add that although the provision of a fourth television channel may not be possible for some time it is our view that the organisational arrangements we have suggested could, in advance, be set up and thus encourage a more systematic approach to educational broadcasting than is possible under present arrangements.

Should you wish me to elaborate on any of the points made in this letter I would be very willing to make myself available. Alternatively, if you would prefer to meet with a small group from the Committee to hear their views at first hand I would be very happy to make the necessary arrangements.

Yours sincerely

K J W ALEXANDER
CHAIRMAN
COMMITTEE ON ADULT EDUCATION IN SCOTLAND

Secretary of State
for Scotland

Scottish Office
Whitehall London SW1A 2AU
6 May 1974

Professor K J W Alexander
Chairman
Committee on Adult Education in Scotland
Department of Economics
Stenhouse Buildings
173 Cathedral Street
GLASGOW
G4 0RQ

Dear Professor Alexander

I am now able to write to you more fully following my Private Secretary's letter of 23 April.

As I am sure you will have noted the Home Secretary made an announcement in Parliament on 10 April about the setting up of a Committee of Enquiry into the future of Broadcasting. The announcement was made in answer to a Parliamentary Question and the terms of reference of the Committee were set out as follows :

> To consider the future of the broadcasting services in the United Kingdom, including the dissemination by wire of broadcast and other programmes and of television for public showing ; to consider the implications for present or any recommended additional services of new techniques ; and to propose what constitutional, organisational and financial arrangements and what conditions should apply to the conduct of all these services.

I have been in touch with Roy Jenkins to see whether they envisage that this Committee would be addressing itself to the kind of points which are dealt with in your letter. They have confirmed to us that they expect the Committee to cover the general field of concern to you about the demand for educational programmes and the implications of this for the allocation of channels.

One of the points you raise is of course specifically about the machinery for administering and exercising control over educational broadcasting. Since responsibility for broadcasting policy rests with the Home Secretary rather than me I have arranged for your letter to be passed to the Office of the Minister of State at the Home Office (Lord Harris) who exercises this responsibility under the Home Secretary. In this way your Committee's view both on the general educational aspects of broadcasting and on the appropriate machinery for handling and controlling educational broadcasting can be given the most effective consideration by the Government.

Sincerely

William Ross

APPENDIX XVIII

Organisations and Individuals who Submitted Written Evidence

(Those marked with an asterisk also gave oral evidence)

Aberdeen Chamber of Commerce
*An Comunn Gaidhealach
Anderson D
*Ashley B J
*Association of County Councils in Scotland
*Association of Directors of Education in Scotland
*Association of Directors of Social Work
*Association of Further Education Officers in Scotland

*Association of Principals of Technical Institutions
Association of University Teachers (Scotland)
Atkinson A M MBE

Banffshire Federation of Community Halls and Associations
Barclay Dr J B
Brand Dr J A
*British Broadcasting Corporation
Brown M

Caplan C
Catholic Education Commission
*Carus R
Ceramics Glass and Mineral Products Industrial Training Board
Chisholm J
Civil Service Council for Further Education
Committee on Education and the Countryside
Co-operative Union Limited
Confederation for the Advancement of State Education
Confederation for the Advancement of State Education (Glasgow Study Group)
Consumer Council
Council for British Archaeology (Scottish Regional Group)
Council for Museums and Galleries in Scotland
Cowper H E and Donnachie I
Currie Further Education Centre, Midlothian

Davies Mrs W
Dow J A

Edinburgh Esperanto Society
*Educational Institute of Scotland
Elgin Society
Elliott R S

Ferguson C D
Fife Education Committee
Forbes Mrs J C

Geddes J C
Grampian Television

Henry H
*Highlands and Islands Development Board
Horticultural Education Association (Scottish Branch)
Hughson Miss M

*Independent Broadcasting Authority
Irvine Development Corporation

Kay J
Kimber Dr I M
Kimber Dr I M and Wood Mrs R

*Landsborough T E M
Lannon T

MacNair T M
Moffat G
Moray House College of Education
Munro H C

National Marriage Guidance Council (Scottish Committee)
National Union of Townswomen's Guilds
*Newbattle Abbey College

Paterson J L
Proudfoot Mrs C

Scottish Association for the Deaf
Scottish Association of Flower Arrangement Societies
*Scottish Association for Liberal Education
Scottish Central Committee for Adult Education in HM Forces
Scottish Civic Trust
Scottish Committee for the Welfare of the Disabled (The Education and Employment Panel)
Scottish Council of the Labour Party
Scottish Council of Physical Recreation
*Scottish Counties of Cities Association
Scottish Episcopal Church
Scottish Field Studies Association
*Scottish Institute of Adult Education
Scottish Liberal Party
Scottish Library Association
Scottish National Camps Association Limited
Scottish Pre-School Playgroup Association
Scottish Schoolmasters Association
Scottish Standing Conference of Voluntary Youth Organisations
*Scottish Television Limited
*Scottish Trades Union Congress (General Council)
Scottish Women's Rural Institutes
Skinner T W
Smith J
*Social Work Services Group, Scottish Education Department
Society of Industrial Tutors
*South-East Scotland Branch of the Association of Tutors in Adult Education
*Standing Consultative Council on Youth and Community Service
Summers A

Titmus C J

University of Aberdeen Extra-Mural Department
University of Dundee
University of Dundee Extra-Mural Committee for Adult Education
University of Edinburgh Department of Adult Education and Extra-Mural Studies
University of Glasgow
University of St Andrews
University of St Andrews Consultative Committee for Extra-Mural Education
*University of Strathclyde

Wassell R P
Welsh M E
Workers' Educational Association (Kirkcaldy Branch)
*Workers' Educational Association (Scottish Council)

APPENDIX XIX

Organisations and Individuals who gave Oral Evidence only

Anderson Sir W Ferguson Professor of Geriatrics University of Glasgow
Director of Education, Inverness Education Authority
Director of Education, Ross and Cromarty Education Authority
Director of Education, Sutherland Education Authority
Director of Extra-Mural Studies, University of Aberdeen
Director of Extra-Mural Studies, University of Dundee
Director of Extra-Mural Studies, University of Edinburgh
Director of Extra-Mural Studies, University of Glasgow
Director of Extra-Mural Studies, University of St Andrews

Jackson K (Department of Adult Education and Extra-Mural Studies, University of Liverpool)
McIver T
Mackay D G Scottish Development Department
Nicholls Dr D (Department of Town and Regional Planning, University of Glasgow)
Reith Dr G (Chairman, Standing Consultative Council on Youth and Community Service)
Scottish Home and Health Department, Prisons Division

APPENDIX XX

Visits made by Members of the Committee

SCOTLAND

Currie Further Education Centre, Midlothian
Lauder Technical College, Fife
Newbattle Abbey Adult Residential College

Borstal Institution, Polmont
HM Prison, Edinburgh
Young Offenders Institution, Barlinnie, Glasgow

Summer Schools:

An Comunn Gaidhealach Summer School, Stornoway, Lewis
Dollar Annual Summer School of the Arts
Festival School, Newbattle Abbey Adult Residential College
Kirkcudbright Summer School in the Arts
Middleton Hall Festival School
Scottish Women's Rural Institutes, Residential School, Edzell
WEA Summer Schools—St Andrews and Tarradale House, Muir of Ord

ENGLAND

Department of Adult Education, University of Keele
Department of Adult Education, University of Leicester
Department of Adult Education, University of Nottingham
Colleges and Further Education Centres in

Derbyshire;
Leicestershire;
Surrey;
West Riding of Yorkshire; and
Inner London

Burton Manor Residential College for Adult Education, Wirral, Cheshire
Fircroft Residential College, Selly Oak, Birmingham
The Old Rectory and White House College, Conference House, Fittleworth, Pulborough, Sussex

OVERSEAS

Finland
Sweden

APPENDIX XXI

Conferences Etc at which the Committee were Represented

Anglo—French Seminar on Adult Education, Paris—May/June 1973

Annual Conference of the Association of Principals of Short-Term Residential Colleges, Horncastle—May 1972

Conference on Industrial Studies, Glasgow University Extra-Mural Department—November 1972

International Conference of University Adult Education, Middleton Hall, Midlothian— November 1972

Scottish Institute of Adult Education Annual Conference—1970–73

Seminar on Adult Education and Community Development at Liverpool—June 1972

Seminar on Innovation in Adult Education, Edinburgh University Extra-Mural Department— May 1971

UNESCO Third World Conference on Adult Education—Tokyo, Japan—August 1972

Workers' Educational Association Conferences—1971–1973

Printed in Scotland by Her Majesty's Stationery Office at HMSO Press, Edinburgh
Dd 960733/3428 K36 2/75 (12043)